more
sand
in
My Bra

funny women write from the road, again

more
sand
in
My Bra

funny women write from the road, again

Edited by
JULIA WEILER and JENNIFER L. LEO

TRAVELERS' TALES

AN IMPRINT OF SOLAS HOUSE

PALO ALTO

Art Direction: Stefan Gutermuth
Cover photograph: © Dominic DeFazio
Page layout: Cynthia Lamb

Library of Congress Cataloging-in-Publication Data

More sand in my bra: funny women write from the road, again / edited by Julia Weiler and Jennifer L. Leo — 1st ed.
    p. cm.
  ISBN 1-932361-50-2 (pbk.)
  1. Women travelers—Anecdotes. 2. Voyages and travels—Anecdotes. 3. Women travelers—humor. 4. Voyages and travels—Humor. I. Weiler, Julia. II. Leo, Jennifer.
  G465.M657 2007
  910.4—dc22

2007012438

First Edition
Printed in the United States
10 9 8 7 6 5 4 3 2 1

*For all the women who've hit the road just a little **too** hard,*

and still gone back for more.

Table of Contents

ix

Introduction

Travel dreams are often born from the most innocuous secrets. I'm quick to credit Tim Cahill as the inspiration for my love of the travel-writing world. But when I was plotting how to break into a men-only adventurer's club in the heart of an aging Los Angeles neighborhood, the roots of my passion came rushing back.

My secret came from my pre-teen years, when I maintained a constant hunger for thrilling, romance-filled movies. I was barely wearing a training bra when *Raiders of the Lost Ark* came out, and had I owned a stick of eyeliner my lids would have been professing my love for Indiana Jones, too. *Romancing the Stone* released when I was in seventh grade and immediately filled my fantasies with notions of love travel. The scene where Michael Douglas surprises Kathleen Turner with a new white dress, and then takes her dancing beneath colored lights at a Colombian street party, left me aching for my first real kiss. Throughout my teens more and more adventure flicks grabbed my heart and imagination, but it was Meryl Streep as the tenacious Karen Blixen in *Out of Africa* that left a permanent impression. From her steadfast dedication to her Kenyan coffee plantation to the love-swept safari nights with Robert Redford—I've had romantic notions of travel for as long as I can remember.

So there I was walking up the stairs and into The Adventurer's Club, hoping I could be just like Baroness

Blixen in the scene where the men who previously shunned her for being a woman opened their exclusive doors and offered her a drink. Nothing could have made me want to climb the flight of stairs to the second floor faster than a rule stating that I and my breasts weren't allowed. I was there with Rolf Potts, who was giving a speech on behalf of the Land Rover Drive Around the World expedition, but club members weren't going to give any special allowances for something as trifling as an alleged friendship. No, The Adventurer's Club was serious business.

At the top of the stairs, the lobby was something to behold. A giant stuffed polar bear in a fighting stance shot me a menacing look that suggested I stay where I was. More hunting trophies, antique oil paintings of raucous sea voyages, vintage kayaks, climbing tools, and other age-old gear adorned the walls. The archives of the club dates back to 1921 but the feel of history just in the immediate entryway was enough to humble any journeyman or woman. While the decision-making board members convened in another room to decide my fate that night, I thought about the adventures I still dreamed of taking and the ones that I've read about in these books.

As you know, we've built our women's humor series on making you laugh. In *Sand in My Bra*, *Whose Panties Are These?*, and *The Thong Also Rises*, we took you from horrifying honeymoons and globetrotting calamities to embarrassing encounters on both sides of the border. We included innocent yet challenging travel experiences told by women who just couldn't *and wouldn't* say no to the open road, and then answered the call of the wild by adding men to our lineup in *What Color Is Your Jockstrap?* You'd think that with more than 125 stories of dream trips gone amok we'd covered it all.

We've been there and done that on all the continents and in the seas and airspace in between. But the wonderful thing about the world is just how darn big and rich it is in possibilities for adventure and misadventure—and more great stories. Hence this book.

For the past five years I've toured the nation to meet our fans, create new ones, and speak about what is so wonderfully compelling about travel—and especially travel gone wrong. What I found in the audiences from Seattle, Washington, to Atlanta, Georgia, were two types of people: women looking for just a little more inspiration, if not an outright O.K. to get out there and fulfill their travel dreams; and travelers who have experienced the wonders of transformation for having stepped out the door, and wanted to share the joy with their friends or family. I was told over and over again that our women's series had helped travelers who needed that extra nudge—the confidence in knowing that "If that happened to her and she lived to laugh about it—I can too!"

Our newest title, *More Sand in My Bra,* returns to the name of our original muse. But lest you think we are regurgitating the same laugh over and over, here's reason to pause. The biggest and best addition to the series is Julia Weiler, who compiled the collection before you. True fans of the series will recognize Julia's name instantly. I first met her when she answered our call to the Fancy Pants Contest, and won it with her Traveler's Utili-Panties. She then went on to contribute gut-clenching stories to both *Thong* and *Jockstrap.* I chose Julia to take over editing the series because she has the most amazing ability to combine an adventurous spirit with genuine grace. She is daring and ready to step out on the most precarious back roads while also remaining flawlessly feminine.

Julia proves that a woman can be both adventurous *and* pretty, whether wearing worn-out jeans or a flowing skirt.

So, it's no surprise that her selections for *More Sand in My Bra* embody loads of inspiration. The stories within do more than just joke about bad trips— they give us far more reason to embrace our inner travel maven. This book is just what the fans have been asking for—stories that motivate us to get our butts off the daydreaming couch and onto spinning wishes into reality.

In "Oh, the Places She Will Go," Rachel Thurston gives us a peek at her childhood and teaches us that staying true to our travel spirit can sometimes mean swimming up society's thick, muddy, stream—but in the end, it's worth it. Suzanne Schlosberg's "Lost in Sex Camp" illustrates that even the seemingly idyllic Club Med vacation can make one question their definition of travel nirvana. Ellen fans, including myself, will laugh at anything she writes even if it's simply her notes from a comedy tour in "Dear Diary." If you, or one of your friends, need the extra push out the door please read "Once That Gun Goes Off" by Laura Katers, and take Beth Martinson's fortitude to heart when you find that those you love just don't get why every place else seems more interesting than home. That said, Jane Hannon proves to us that not every adventure should be taken, especially when it involves getting a bikini wax in Vietnam.

The members of The Adventurer's Club returned and offered me a friendly welcome to their meeting. I had done it, made it through the exclusivity clause without having been to more than 150 countries, climbed Mount Everest, or rafted down a Class V rapid. I excitedly moved from room to room and found a hallway lined with portraits of past club presidents leading to the main auditorium. This was where they convened to hear the inspiring tales of other adventurers, and share their own. The room had a high arched ceiling and the decor was even more elaborate than the lobby. On this particular night there was someone more interesting than the guest speaker in the house: John Goddard. Sometimes called "The Real Indiana Jones," Goddard is famous for his "Life List," 127 adventurous goals he wrote down when he was 15. More than sixty years later he's completed 109 of them, including a wide variety of explorations and accomplishments from learning languages and flying planes to swimming in numerous seas, climbing the world's most famous mountains, photographing best-loved waterfalls, milking a poisonous snake, studying primitive cultures, and more or less experiencing life to the fullest all over the world. His list remains on the wall in their dining hall and provided enough inspiration for several nights to come.

I reminded myself then, it doesn't matter how far you travel or who you travel with—just that you leave your comfort zone for a few moments to see what the world looks like from a different view. That's what we've been trying to say by doing this series of books, and the women who've shared their stories have shown us that tenfold. We read about their adventures and watch from the sidelines in the comfort of our own bathtub, chaise lounge, comfy chair, or even the economy seat of a plane taking us on our own trip. Do something for me: listen to the voice that tells you why traveling would be so great instead of the voice that tells you to just stay home. The real questions you should be asking yourself are: Where do you want to go next? And when?

—JENNIFER L. LEO
Pasadena, California

ANNE MERRIGAN

* ✳ *

Come Here

She put on a one-woman show.

"COME HERE. COME HERE," THE LITTLE MAN BY THE ocean calls.

Glancing behind me, I'm alone. *Me? Does he mean me?*

"Over here. Over here." His voice rises above the waves. The man's tweed cap is slung low over his forehead. He's squatting while staring into a tide pool.

I shrug and descend the path. It's my annual weekend at the ocean honoring myself, leaving behind life's responsibilities, and reclaiming my own rhythms.

"See there," he points excitedly at a group of starfish. "They're ready to spawn."

"Spawn?"

"Have sex," he clarifies. "The male starfish spawn gametes which—"

"In a group?" I protest.

"Yes, yes, yes. It increases their chances of fertilization. They use environmental signals to…"

Is he a pervert? No, he's more like a professor.

"Come here. Come here," he repeats head down, sensing

another presence on the path. I pass a couple as I ascend the rocks; now, with numbing doubts. Starfish are enjoying an orgy, and I'm single. Plenty of fish in the ocean—ha! The romantic fish I've encountered have passed their expiration date, and all deserved to be fried in hot oil. Repressing my disillusionment, I breathe deeply of ocean smells, the roar of the waves soothing my spirit, restoring calm.

Returning to my third-floor motel room, I have a light supper, basking in a full ocean view. The establishment sports an indoor pool with an adult swim from 9 to 10 P.M. nightly. I relax in the Jacuzzi following an evening of uninterrupted reading. My body feels like liquid satin as I prepare for bed, peacefully drifting asleep.

A loud noise awakens me. Sitting up confused, I wonder if someone's at the door. The banging continues from behind me. Enlightenment surfaces; the couple next door are intimately entwined. *Great! Just great!* I lie down, feeling like a voyeur to their lovemaking. Grunts and groans reverberate at a rapid pace. The shrill of a train whistle sounds. I bolt up. *There's a train nearby?* Good God, it's the woman! Boy, she clutches a note. Enough already! I resist pounding on the wall. Eventually, her steam vaporizes. The spawning is over. Sleep overcomes me.

Struggling out of an unconscious state, noises resound an hour later. Not again! My inner peace sanctum Rabbit vibrator could not keep this pace. Oh, no! They're coming from the opposite wall. A man's voice…. "Oh, baby" repeats like a broken record; the utterances rise and fall like scales on the piano. *What the hell is she performing on him?* Wishing to lend him a thesaurus, I restrain from throwing a shoe against the wall. Silence falls an hour later. The inner turmoil of my single status leads to a troubled sleep.

Rising late the following morning, I enjoy a leisure-filled day of walking beaches, exploring little shops, and eating homemade sweets. During the adult swim, a young couple strolls in laughing. The woman wears a bridesmaid gown, the man a tux. The pair grabs the undivided attention of the middle-age crew in the Jacuzzi when they undress. The woman reveals a bikini underneath, the man strips to his thong. He hops in beside me as his date descends the steps. "How ya doing?" he asks me. Speechless, I stare at his well defined six-pack. *I'm sitting next to an unknown hunk in his underwear. Why am I surprised?* "Who got married?" someone asks. A conversation begins about the pitfalls of relationships.

Upon returning to my room, uninterrupted sleep beckons me. I surrender,

——)——

The air started leaking out of my mattress while I was camping one night, but I was too cozy and warm to go looking for the "turtle." The turtle is what I call my blue mattress pump because it is shaped like the little reptile. Later that evening, I awoke to the familiar sound of air being pumped into a mattress, so when I got up in the morning I said to my cousin and her husband, "You must have lost the air in your mattresses, too." They shot me a quizzical look and a shrug so I continued, "I heard you pumping the turtle last night."

"Oh?" she asked. "OH!!!" Suddenly my cousin had a quite shocked, embarrassed look on her face as they apparently don't talk about such things in mixed company. To this day, we refer to certain activities as "pumping the turtle."

◆

—Louise Schutte,
"Pumping the Turtle"

dreaming of the wind moaning and the cries of seagulls, except—realization slowly dawns—both rooms are fully engaged. My innate power energizes me like a wave crashing
on the beach. I unfurl myself, standing upright, holding my
vibrator high like a torch. Single women unite! I enjoy my
own company. I can nourish myself without infringing on
others' hearing. The noises emitting from both rooms
crescendo into a XXX-rated movie. I take action.

Grabbing the desk chair, I place it against the wall, banging its top repeatedly while pressing the vibrator to the wall
in a circular motion, shouting, "Holy moley, do it again!
Harder! Tie me tighter. Use the whip!" I pick up the chair
darting to the opposite wall, repeating the performance.
Back and forth I move for a full five minutes. Upon stopping, absolute silence reigns.

I blast the shower to disguise my belly laughs. Two souls
are not required for my creative spirit to swell. Proud of my
emotional maturity, I sleep like a baby.

*Anne Merrigan is a therapist who loves to tell a tale. The accomplish-
ment she is most proud of is receiving her scuba diving certification.
She completed her check-out dives on her forty-third birthday at a
depth of forty feet and still enjoys breathing underwater to this day.
Anne has been known to break up starfish orgies when she encounters them on her dives, especially when she has had the recent need to
perform her one-woman act. She feels no guilt about this, and sleeps
like an infant afterwards.*

* ✷ *

Booty Call

If the shoe fits, then you
just might be a pirate.

"I WANT TO GO HOME," JAMIE SAID AS SHE LOOKED AT me and pouted. "I'm having a rotten time here. Let's just go. We clearly don't belong!"

I was stunned. We had been in San Francisco only for a matter of minutes—only long enough to check into our hotel room—and already she wanted to leave.

"But we come here every year for our birthdays and we always have a great time," I argued. "Just relax. We'll get settled and then head over to get a cookie from the French bakery around the corner."

"I don't want to go anywhere," Jamie asserted. "I'm too embarrassed. Didn't you see as we drove up that every single woman in San Francisco had amazing black leather boots on? Every single one, except two: you and me. We're going to stand out like sore thumbs. Everyone will know we're tourists and the street people will hit us up for money even more."

I laughed. "You're upset because we don't have black boots? You're forgetting that the French bakery isn't the only reason we stay in this hotel. It's also because of the great Indian food joint around the corner, the incredible breakfast place down the street, the free croissants and doughnuts in the morning by the coffee machine, *and*," I said, pointing out the window, "the largest designer shoe warehouse in all of San Francisco, proudly boasting three floors of nothing but discount high-end footwear, visible right now through that window."

"Oh my God," Jamie gasped as she covered her mouth. "Look! I see boots! Rows and rows of nothing but black boots! If there was a sign that said 'Free!' or even '75% Off Our Already Incredibly Low Prices' I would think we had died and maybe weren't such selfish, shallow people after all!"

"I know," I said, nodding my head and looking across the street. "Cheap, cool shoes. That's as close to heaven as you can get. Let's go. My buzz from the drinks on the plane is wearing off, and if there's anything I loathe more than religion and taxes, it's another woman touching the shoes that I want."

As we entered the store, both Jamie and I gasped with amazement, overwhelmed by the vast variety of choices. There were black boots everywhere, lined up along every top shelf, like spires on a castle. We dove in hungrily, tossing our purses aside and grabbing every long boot box in our size. Jamie, the more coordinated of the two of us, was the first to kick off her sneakers and slide her foot into a glorious, shiny tall boot. I was right behind her, whipping off a shoe and getting ready to ram my foot into a pair of my own when I heard a sharp cry and realized it was coming from my friend.

"I can't get it up!" she cried. "I can't get this zipper up! It won't fit! This boot won't fit!"

"Well, it must be broken," I said, eager to see myself walking around in my own pair of black San Francisco native boots. "Try the other one."

"I did!" Jamie shot back. "I can't get that one up, either!"

"Then get the next size up," I replied, as I pulled the zipper on my pair of boots, which worked absolutely, perfectly, fabulously fine until it reached the middle of my leg.

"It's not my foot that doesn't fit," Jamie whispered harshly. "It's...my...*calf!*"

"You mean it's our *calves*," I informed her while my fingers were turning purple with bruises and blood clots trying to force the boot zipper over the state fair-winning watermelon that had apparently seeded and grown between my knee and ankle.

I turned to look at Jamie, who was staring at me with her mouth hanging open all the way to the top of her unzipped boots.

"Fatty calves," we whispered to each other. "Calf bloat!"

We couldn't believe it. When had this happened? *How* had it happened? How do you just wake up one day and find your last flattering feature has deserted you like a guy who freaks out the first time you bring a stick of your deodorant to his house? I suppose, however, that there were signs. Signs such as the time I was trying to tie my shoe and my very own fat tube bucked backward with a reverse roll into my abdomen and completely bit me; signs such as the instant that I looked in the mirror and saw Tipper Gore's neck underneath my head; signs such as our only party motto was "If you lose me, look for the cheese platter"; or the sign of how I pledged my loyalty to the Awesome Blossom despite the fact that I received, and read, the mass e-mail that said it contained 300 grams of fat. Looking back, I suppose it was only a matter of time before the trickle-down theory was applied to the excess of my paunch and began to distribute itself evenly to my few remaining skinny parts, like my knuckles, earlobes, and now, apparently, my calves.

Indeed, the realization that fatty calves had assumed resident status on our legs was a chilling moment and in hindsight ranked in third place in my list of Horrifying Moments of Truth in my life, preceded only by:

The Second Most Horrifying Moment of Truth, 11:53 P.M., October 5, 1999: Previously, I could have sworn that every kernel of the Dripping with Butter at the Movies Microwave Popcorn that I was addicted to had been individually kissed by butter angels had I not once accidentally opened a prepopped packet of butter-marinated popcorn and seen the horror inside for myself. There, lying quietly inside the bag, was an orange gelatinous puddle the color of sinister toxic waste and the consistency of a bar of Irish Spring. It looked as if someone had melted, then solidified, Ronald McDonald and squirted him into bags of kernels. It was vile. It was unnatural. It was definitely cancer. Don't get me wrong, it tasted great when the popping was all said and done, but it was kind of like unexpectedly seeing your mom naked. It was the brand of truth you shouldn't even attempt to handle yourself without the aid of a skilled professional, and I firmly believe that stuff should be renamed "At the Movies in Chernobyl" Microwave Popcorn.

The First and Most Paramount Horrifying Moment of Truth, 10:47 A.M., May 2, 1978: I permitted Kay, a stoner chick and the only person who would talk to me in Beginning Choir at Shea Middle School, to look into my eighth-grade clutch purse for a stick of gum because her breath reeked of the joint she had just consumed by herself.

I watched helplessly as her hand emerged from my purse, not with a stick of gum, but with the toothbrush that I had to carry because of my braces, which now had the exposed strip of a maxi pad stuck to it. With the handle of the toothbrush in her hand, she raised it up above her head and proceeded to run around the classroom like it was an American flag as she chanted, "Whorie Laurie! Whorie Laurie!"

And now, a new, amazing prolific achievement of my life rolled in as Fatty Calf Syndrome, possibly bumping the Chernobyl popcorn incident.

"What can we do about our enormous bulging calves?" I asked Jamie in a panic. "A calf-reduction procedure? Deaugmentation? Leg liposuction? Little rubber fat suits from the knee down? How do I put my calves on a diet? What do we do? *What* do *we* do?!!!"

"What we're going to do," Jamie said, leaning in and furrowing her brow in a definite badge of determination, "is find boots to fit our freakishly large Laura Bush legs. We're in San Francisco, the capital of the world for men, with big men legs, who live to shop for and wear ladies' clothing. There's bound to be a transvestite store somewhere within five square miles that sells boots that our basketball calves can fit into!"

So we embarked on our hunt for the entire rest of the day, scouting out any store windows displaying rubber dresses, clothing with an inordinate amount of sequins, and any Wonder Woman outfits or memorabilia whatsoever. But after we hit eight shoe stores with not one pair that would fit us and one she-male boutique that only carried slippers that were the size of pontoon boats alluringly adorned with pink feathers, we still came up empty-calved, with the exception of a pair of very firm and perky attachable breast forms in case I ever have to start dating again.

I was about to give up when a man named Destiny who had thinner legs and nicer cheekbones than we did overheard our plight at Uncanny Tranny and directed us to a place he said could probably help us.

"I don't know if I can withstand the humiliation of another store," I whined. "Frankly, I think I'd rather play with generic whiskey and a bunch of knives."

"One last store," Jamie gasped as we tried to make it up another steep San Francisco hill. "If we don't succeed this time, I promise we can go back to the hotel room and lie down until our calves atrophy and our bodies eventually absorb them."

"How can I help you?" the cordial shoe man said as soon as we entered the store.

"Someone took half my ass and stuck it under my knee," Jamie said, breathing heavily and pointing to her stout, engorged calf. "And I am not going back out there until I can fit a boot around them."

"And I apparently have Christina Ricci's blow-pop head emerging from behind either of my shins," I added, pointing to my leg loaves. "Oh my God. Either those are cellulite potholes or they're forming sockets for eyes!"

"This happens a lot," the jolly shoe man said as he emitted a deep, heavy sigh and shook his head. "Active ladies like yourselves often pay a price for their athletic lifestyles, and I'm afraid this is one of the tolls. Boot manufacturers make boots sized for models—but models don't walk, they have drivers! They're lazy skinny people! It's a horrible side effect of having such a finely sculptured calf, as opposed to a flat, flappy supermodel one."

"You are so right!" Jamie gushed. "Who wants a pancake for a calf when you can have a Cinnabon? This calf shows the dedication to my sport, even if I really haven't considered taking one up yet!"

"I have a hobby," I volunteered meekly. "It's chicken fried steak."

"I have just the boots for you!" he said as he snapped his fingers and disappeared into the back room.

Now, true, he was using the term "athletic" as loosely as the skin that's gathered like drapes around Elizabeth Taylor's head, but frankly, I didn't care. If he wanted to pretend that our calves were well developed rather than identify them as the lumps of cellulite and homes to a lifetime of Hostess Ding Dong toxic waste deposits that they really were, I was totally into it. He had earned his commission from me, and if there was any way he was willing to point out the firmness of my rock-in-a-sock boobs, I'd kick in another five bucks as well.

Honestly, I don't know what I expected from a man who would lie straight to my double chin and John Goodman neck and tell me that I looked "athletic," but I did expect something more than what I saw when he opened the two boxes of boots and presented us with his fat-calf bounty.

Jamie was the first to speak. "Wow," she said slowly and quietly. "Are those...pirate boots?"

"Well, let's just say they have a swarthy influence to them," the exuberant shoe man glowed. "Aren't they wonderful?"

"Sure, if I had some pieces of eight and a hook hand to go with them," I said, staring at the big silver buckle and the way they folded over the top.

"And perhaps a parrot and a peg leg," Jamie added as she picked up one of the boots from her box and began to try it on.

"These are the only boots you have?" I asked.

The friendly shoe man nodded. "And these are the last two pairs in your size," he added.

"I'll take them," Jamie said as she walked around the store with them, looking as if she was about to pillage a schooner.

"Oh, all right, I'll take them, too," I said, but only after I was sure they could swallow and digest my bulbous leg mushrooms. "At least if I know that when I'm short on money, I can either get hooked up at the Pirates of the Caribbean or a community theater production of *Peter Pan*."

As the friendly shoe man was swiping our VISA cards and thanking God Almighty that he had finally unloaded inventory that had sat on his shelf since Adam Ant still had a career, I turned to my friend, Captain Ahab.

"We're going to look like assholes, you know," I said.

"I know," she answered. "But at least we'll look like *native* assholes. Ahoy, matey."

Laurie Notaro was born in New York, raised in Arizona, and now calls Eugene, Oregon home. She is the author of the New York Times *bestseller* The Idiot Girls' Action–Adventure Club, *as well as many other titles* including There's a (Slight) Chance I Might Be Going to Hell: A Novel of Sewer Pipes, Pageant Queens, and Big Trouble, I Love Everybody (and other atrocious lies), *and* We Thought You Would Be Prettier, *from which this story was excerpted.*

*

All over Southeast Asia, teeny-tiny women everywhere are strapping portable mini-stages to their feet and calling them shoes. These otherwise sensible-looking ladies have apparently deemed it fashionable to perch themselves on these precarious platforms, these six inch soles of certain death, and proceed to walk around in them as though it was perfectly natural to wear stilts casually. It seemed ridiculous, and it seemed to defy both gravity and logic. Still, there seemed to be something to it.

I had to know what these women knew. Would platform shoes transform me into a Travolta-like disco queen? Would I slip them on and suddenly have a better sense of the weather? Would these towering soles built of cork, rubber, leather, spangles, ribbon… and whatever else was readily available, lift me closer to God?

I spotted a pair at the market in my size and knew I had to try them on. How hard could it be? After all, I'd seen women in platforms walking on the beach, hiking in the jungle, trekking up a hill…they were worn for all occasions! I slipped off my oh-so practical Tevas and stepped up into the über-tall shoes.

Suddenly—I was elevated to never-before-experienced vantages. I was super model height…I was…Heidi Klum! I was Super-Duper High Girl. *I could look down my nose at my husband.* I was hooked… even after I took my first unfortunate step. I won't say what happened next, just that a skinned knee here, a little bruise there is really just a small price to pay for all that instant stature. Walking is overrated anyways. Still, I'm practicing, and even though I'll probably never glide as gracefully as those gals in Southeast Asia, I'm getting better at making it across the room.

— Julia Weiler, "Exploring New Heights"

* ✳ *

Thar She Blows!

She went above and beyond the call of doody.

THEY SAY THE JOURNEY OF A THOUSAND MILES—OR seventeen thousand miles as the case may be—begins with one step. It was our honeymoon and we would travel from Seattle to the South Pacific to Hong Kong via thirty-five-foot sailboat. People said if our fledgling marriage could survive this, it would survive anything. But what does it mean when that proverbial first step, that decisive heel-toe, that inertia-shattering clomp lands squarely in shit?

Shoving off the dock that first morning felt exhilarating and momentous. Behind the wheel in my snappy white sneakers, my hair blowing in the breeze, I was the model in the tampon ad—I was *Carefree!* We'd quit our jobs, sold the cars, rented the house. For the past week we'd been living aboard, getting the final preparations done for our big trip. And now, I beamed, we were finally setting sail. But, my newlywed husband Graeme reminded me, before we could set the sails, before we could even leave the harbor, we had to stop and pump the head.

First, a little terminology. The "head" on a sailboat isn't, as one might think, the top of the mast or the nose of the boat or some *Starship Enterprise*-like command center. No, the head of a sailboat is its toilet (a telling linguistic linkage that I should have taken as an omen). The head leads to the holding tank, which is where, in the United States at least, boats are required to store sewage until either a) they travel sufficiently far from land to dump it overboard, or b) they dock at an über-sized port-a-potty where they can pump it out. As an aside, travelers in search of turquoise waters should be warned that not a single country between the U.S. and Hong Kong asked us to use a pump-out station—indeed, most countries outside the U.S. don't *have* pump-out stations. That brown floatie thing you encountered while snorkeling among the pretty sailboats in Cabo last year? Not a candy bar.

But, as I was saying, our holding tank was chockablock full (we'd been eating at the marina's greasy fish 'n' chips shop for a week now), and it would be another week before we'd be far enough away from land to dump. So our first step was to offload our crap.

The water was as gray as the weather. The marina was quiet except for the occasional seagull's squawk. At six A.M., the live-aboard community was still snug in bed, so Graeme and I used our silent directional hand signals as we ghosted toward the pump-out station. We were good enough at docking by now that I didn't have to use the most expressive hand signal I know, the one named after the gull sitting on the piling nearby; though it would come in handy soon enough. We secured the dock lines and I donned my heavy-duty orange rubber gloves with a snap. I clambered on deck, unscrewed the cap to the holding tank, and peered into the bowels of the boat.

Now you may wonder why I, the blushing bride in the tidy tank top and the bright white Keds, was the one hovering over the tank of poo, while my captainly husband cowered on the dock as far away from the anus-like opening as he could get. Graeme, a man who will wear the same boxer shorts for days at a time, who has tested various forms of foliage for their ass-wiping qualities on long morning jogs (dare I say runs?), and who once even caught in his bare hands his drunken friend's fresh turd tossed to him while swimming in the Taiwanese Strait (the only warning being, "Here! Catch!"), has an incongruously intense aversion to shit. Then again, maybe it was this last incident that scarred him. Anyway, I had learned long ago that any job involving feces (cleaning the toilet, picking up dog poop, fixing the head) resulted in melodramatic nose-pinching, reflexive gagging, and incessant bitching. It was I who would have to take this job, as it were, head-on.

Standing on the dock, his nose turned away in disgust, Graeme dangled towards me a long gray hose of variegated plastic. He held it at arm's length like one would a dirty rag or a dead rat or, more to the point, a long gray hose of variegated plastic that is frequently dipped in shit. I grabbed it and stuffed the end in our holding tank. He retreated to the poop-sucking machine and put his hand on the switch. It was time to start pumping.

I gave Graeme the go-ahead. He flipped the switch and the hose in my hands began to vibrate. It made a sound much akin to that which your household vacuum cleaner would make if, instead of flushing, you decided to vacuum out the toilet bowl the morning after the Elk's Club annual chili feed. SSSHLLEEEEWK! Now pretend that your vacuum hose is also blessed, thanks to thoughtful engineering, with a clear plastic section through which you can see the remains of Edna's award-winning chili travel swiftly towards a new home.

I was watching this see-through section of hose with the same morbid fascination with which one pops a big fat zit, when I realized the dang thing was no longer working. Not only had the flow of brown effluent slowed to a trickle, but the pump was making an angry whining sound. I pushed the hose into the hole harder. No good. I wiggled it back and forth. Still no poop. Yet I knew the tank couldn't possibly be empty as I'd only been sucking for a minute or two. With one hand holding the hose in place, I waved to Graeme and ran my orange glove across my neck—cut it. Graeme turned off the machine. Graeme scratched his head. Graeme tapped his foot. Then he suggested that we put some fresh water *into* the tank in order to clean it and push out the stuff we knew was still there. Kind of like a sailboat enema. Unable, in that brief moment, to conjure any logical objections, I inserted the water hose into the water hole, which was, quite logically just in front of the poop hole, and returned my hands to the poop hose, which I held firmly in place. Graeme turned on the water spigot and prepared to switch the pump on again. "Ready?" I nodded.

Have you ever taken a good long swig of Coca-Cola right before your best friend makes you laugh hysterically? Have you witnessed the force of a fire hose let loose on a burning building? Have you visited the geysers at Yellowstone National Park? We're talking Old Faithful here. That shit shot sky high and landed EVERYWHERE—on the boat, on the dock, on Graeme, on the seagull sitting on the piling, and most particularly on ME! My tank top was no longer tidy, my shoes no longer white. My shrieks rose like a siren, waking every creature, living and dead, within five counties. "Omigod! OH MY GAWD! OOHH MYYY GAAAWD!" Shit dripped down my hair. Shit clogged my ears. Shit plastered my eyeglasses. In darkness, I used my index fingers like windshield wipers across my spectacles—back and forth, back and forth—until I could finally see again. Graeme was clutching his belly with one hand, cupping his gagging mouth with the other, as he stared in horror at his newly betrothed bride. I was covered head to toe in crap.

Slowly, deliberately, valiantly, I rotated and raised the middle finger of my right orange glove, now dripping brown, and directed it squarely at my queasy husband. I was less than pleased.

And then, then, Graeme started to smile. "Is that a red pepper flake from last night's dinner?" he sniggered, pointing to a bright red fleck on my forehead. "And there on your shoulder, that's got to be corn." I could see a few kernels sticking in his hair, too. And, since the only other option was to cry, I started giggling as well. Until we were both doubled over, laughing uncontrollably, loud enough to wake the dead.

Soon I was shivering half naked on the pump-out station dock, Graeme's water hose turned on me. As he hosed me down he mused, "Some sort of pressure must have built up when we added the water to the tank." I shrugged, not caring so much how it happened, but how I was going to get this *eau de merde* out of my hair, my nostrils, my ear canals. Once he'd sprayed the thick stuff off, I went down to the head to shower. When I opened the cupboard to get the shampoo, however, I noticed a distressing new development—everything in the cabinet was floating. *Oh crap!* I thought. *We've overflowed down here too!* But on closer inspection, the cabinet was filled with water, the same clean water we *thought* we'd been putting into the holding tank to induce the sailboat enema. Turns out the water hadn't entered the tank at all. But then what had made her blow?

Returning to the cockpit, I explained the perplexing new discovery to Graeme. He scratched his head and rubbed his chin. Then he grew grave and philosophical. "You know, Janna, we all know shit happens." I rolled my eyes. "And when shit happens," he continued, "I want to be as far away from it as possible."

We haven't used a pump-out station since.

Janna Cawrse is a Seattle-based writer and creator of "Happily Even After," a Seattle Post-Intelligencer *relationship blog for the committed. Her stories have been published in various anthologies including* What Color Is Your Jockstrap? *and* Sweat & the City: Stories and Poems from the Hong Kong Workplace. *She writes for* SAIL, Cruising World, *and* Blue Water Sailing. *Her current book project is part adventure log, part confessional, part love story:* The Motion of the Ocean: love, life and sex on the high seas. *As a new mother, she is currently embarking on further adventures with poo.*

★

The Spa Who Loved Me

*She visited a mutually supportive community
and bared way more than just her soul.*

WHEN FACED WITH GETTING NAKED AROUND NEW people, it's best to disrobe right away—before you really start to get to know each other.

At least that's what my man Marty declared before we headed out for a few days at a hot-springs resort deep in the Oregon woods, a resort where clothing was optional by the hot tubs, and my childhood chum Julie and her nuclear family would be in attendance. Julie, it turned out, echoed Marty's mindset, and so it was that we found ourselves speeding around hairpin turns in the forest to get to the resort soon after arriving at the airport.

Breitenbush Retreat and Conference Center...I'd fantasized about the place for months. Breitenbush is a natural hot-springs destination run by members of a hippie commune deep in the Cascade Mountains. There we'd enjoy two days of living in tiny, geothermally heated cabins, taking yoga and meditation classes, wearing thick robes while flowing languidly about the eighty-eight-acre grounds, consuming organically grown food, lying supine for massages, and all the while listening to the rushing river and staring agog at the huge cedar trees rising up all around us.

At the top of everyone's frontal lobe that first day was the nakedness. Marty and I had both been to nude beaches before, and we agreed the experience was more about being free and natural than it was about looking at others or appearing attractive ourselves. That did not, however, explain why we both worked out like madmen during the two weeks preceding the trip.

Once we arrived at Breitenbush, named for a one-armed man whom some explorer found in the forest way back when, we got settled in our cabins and sat down to a big, communal stir-fry served up by twenty-something people in knee socks and clogs, people with names such as "Free" and "Totem." After digestion, it was time to hit the Sacred Circle, five small hot tubs on a raised deck adjacent to the Breitenbush River. Each tub, said the pamphlet, is hotter than the last; the final one would most accurately be called a "butt-cold" tub. The idea, basically, is to make your vessels do a mean round of push-ups without succumbing to a heart attack.

In the dimming twilight down by the river, the Sacred Circle was abuzz with all types: those bearing dreadlocks and those with bald heads, hairy hippie moms with boobs like rocks in socks, and the young, taut students of a massage school in Seattle. Some spa-goers wore bathing suits, but most didn't. I didn't look at too much of the nakedness at first; I just turned my back on it all, gritted my teeth and pulled off my robe. And in an instant, there I stood amid about twenty-five people on a summer night in Oregon, naked as the day I popped out of my mom. The breeze dancing on my butt felt funny.

I turned around to see Marty pulling off his sweatpants. My pal Julie was already nude and in a tub with her toddler, Siena. That was all cool. But I just couldn't bring myself to look at George, Julie's husband of seven years. Oh sure, when he turned his back on me and made his way from tub to tub, I sneaked peeks at his hind end, but his front? No way. I just couldn't do it—that would have been like stealing peeks at my brother's penis. Ick!

I slipped into a tub with Julie and Siena, and before too long, the recently weaned toddler was diving for my boobs, her hands out in front of her like a plumber eager to work two stubborn nozzles. I subtly batted her away underwater, but the milk-hungry girl would not be deterred. "Is there *noo-noo* in there?" she spouted in front of a tub full of people, all of whom were looking at her and cooing.

"Actually, um, no," I said, feeling like a useless spigot on some abandoned property out by the highway.

I high-tailed it out of there and into the next tub, noting that even though these people were naked as jaybirds, their conversations were remarkably like those that take place around your garden-variety coffee table flanked by people wearing pants. Everyone trained their eyes on everyone else's heads as their mouths yammered on about things such as coastal erosion and foreign affairs.

A small brunette woman suddenly shattered the coffee-table illusion. She thrust her rigid, tattooed body across the expanse of the little tub I was in, and demanded "reflexology" from a man sitting opposite her. All her pertinent parts were on display and very near the water's surface as the man gave her a foot massage. I guess I'd never seen that happen around a coffee table.

In the hottest pool, I met up with Marty and Julie and a jolly Santa Claus-shaped man relating a story about the time he visited some hot springs in Iceland. His eyes sparkled as he bobbed in the water, telling us how the Icelandic spatenders would come in and mumble something like "nickity snikity" when it was time to get out of the springs and jump into a hole in the ice like a pack of walruses. With that, Saint Nick rose up and lumbered over to the cold tub, leaving rollicking waves in his wake.

Julie left, too, and was replaced by a young, rotund Hawaiian man who had arrived at the Sacred Circle in a sarong. He stripped off his colorful skirt and hopped right in going completely under, face down. With no one else in the tub and nothing to talk about, all Marty and I could do was stare at this manatee of a man, wondering when, if ever, he would surface, and hoping against hope that all the bubbles coming up from around his lower midriff area were just trapped air pockets from some unseen vent somewhere.

> ———) ———
>
> I was looking up and down the beach for Cheryl but couldn't find her through the sea of undulating skin. Scanning the happy naked multitudes on the beach without looking like I was staring was a challenge. As my eyes skimmed over the bronzed humans standing, sitting, running about with Frisbees, and so forth, my brain registered what my eyes were finding: penis, penis, umbrella, butt butt butt and penis, boobs, cooler, penis, penis, beer can...Shit! Can't find her.
>
> ◆
>
> —Judy Edwards,
> "Orion's Surprise"

Then, a fully clothed commune member squatted down to take the tub's temperature and announced to us and the submerged man that it was 109 degrees in there. I looked at my waterproof watch and noticed that the face had popped off. I was surprised my own face didn't do the same.

Being a huge wuss about the cold, it was with mortal trepidation that I rose out of the scalding tub and dunked myself into the tub filled with frigid river water. Though in there for only a demi-nanosecond, all my bones felt as if they'd shattered in that instant. Walking around after that, finally I understood what life as a menthol cigarette feels like.

Giddy and spent from the capillary calisthenics, it was tough to drag our asses along the path to the two more natural-looking springs in a nearby sloping mountain meadow. Somehow we pulled it off. We reclined in the hot magma-heated water and stared at the stars along with a few other naked folks and their floating genitals.

Walking back to the cabins, the eerily articulate Siena blurted out, "When I grow up and get boobies and Mommy and Daddy aren't around and I'm in private, can I touch them?"

"Why yes," Julie replied, and in celebration of Siena's future freedom, we retired to the cabins and consumed our contraband Doritos and beer. That night as I slept, I was so zenned-out and blank from the healing waters, I barely felt the Good 'n' Plenty-sized ants crawling on my face. I had become as one with them, and with their huge moth friends, too.

The next day was gorgeous, the sky a crisp blue. At breakfast, Siena got swept up in the free-flowing communal atmosphere. After ingesting her porridge, the tiny girl stood up, declared the crowded deck her stage, and with arms outstretched and eyes closed in deep rapture, she belted out a song. The tune sounded like the theme from *Rocky*, but the words were, "Everybody loves me," repeated over and over again. Then she demanded that each of the adults in her party take turns dancing with her. Thus, I found myself couple-dancing with a two-year-old to the tune of "Gonna Fly Now" while about thirty-five smiling hippies looked on, beaming and clapping. And to think, I did it all without beer.

After that, the boys and Siena took off to hike in the foothills of snowcapped Mount Jefferson, and Julie headed to the Healing Arts Center to get prodded by an Andy Gibb-looking masseuse named Garde. Alone, I thought about taking a Watsu session—the woman on the phone had said this involved getting shoved to and fro in a hot tub—but all the slots were taken. I also wanted to do Evolutionary Spinal Maintenance, which I was told involved standing on one leg while listening to a man tell a meaningful story, but that wasn't until noon.

I decided then to cross the footbridge over the clear, sparkling river and just hang out among the trees. Once I'd crossed the bridge, though, I spied a sign that read PLEASE RESPECT OUR PRIVACY. *Uh-oh,* I thought, *I'm not going to be able to do that.*

My original plan was not to infiltrate—really. I just wanted to find, maybe, a nice rock that jutted into the river, so that I could lie down on it and think about waterfalls and stuff, but once I had reclined on such a rock, all I could think about was worming my way deeper into the commune. How could I not? I'd been nearly obsessed with communes for years, harboring fantasies about how outrageously fulfilling communal living could be. That is… if I'm in charge and have stocked the place with all my closest friends.

But I'd never so much as seen a commune. And lying there under the firs with a commune this close to me, it took me only about ten minutes to gather my stuff and head in for a closer glimpse at Utopia. Hell, the sign said, PLEASE

RESPECT OUR PRIVACY, not KEEP THE FRIG OUT. Respecting one's privacy was subjective, open to interpretation.

And thus I quietly skulked along a trail that seemed to cut right through the center of it all. After a few paces, I saw a ramshackle building with a message board tacked to it that read only: SUNNY BLISS BA HOO BA HOO. On the next building, an open-door cabin that seemed to contain a ratty kitchen, there was a sign that read, BEYOND THIS POINT. Beyond this point what? Beyond this point you must keep going? There weren't any people around to ask, so I figured that's what it meant.

In time, I saw a series of cabins very similar to the rustic one-room jobbies on the other side of the river, only these were much more...lived-in. One had a hammock on the porch next to an amateurish painting of a scantily clad woman. Another porch sported a guitar case and some plants. A tricycle was abandoned in the middle of the path, next to the charred remains of last night's bonfire. And then, just beyond that, there was a large makeshift canvas dome with a sticker of a colorful Buddhist deity on its flappy door. It appeared to be a yoga shack.

As I stood there alone in the eerie quiet, my trespassing experience began to feel akin to visiting Jonestown after the Kool-Aid but before the press got there. Only there weren't any bodies. Not that I could see anyway. I figured for a moment that the residents must be in the yoga dome, lined up flush with each other, and dead as doornails. I was tempted to peek in, but picturing myself dramatically screaming and running down the path arms a-flail after that, I somehow knew that if I looked in there, I'd just interrupt a closed-to-the-public ecstatic dance session and get myself in big trouble. I decided to leave well enough alone.

As I slithered on out of there, I noticed that the parking lot was occupied by just as many Broncos and Fiats as it was Volkswagen buses. For a moment, I was filled with the urge to go back and see what other strange contradictions I could find...VCRs, pearls, guns, or, God forbid, cell phones? I decided that I couldn't afford all the bad karma that might produce.

Back on the legal side of the river, I stopped into the small gift shop/resort office to admire the meditation CDs and tarot cards. I was leafing through *The Runemaster's Handbook* when I heard a crisis unraveling behind me. Through crackly static, a girl's voice came in over a walkie-talkie.

"Hello, Free?"

"Yes," said Free, a gaunt and disheveled boy in a skirt.

"Free, I seem to have broken the water fountain. Water is shooting everywhere," said the alarmed voice.

"Nova, this is a day of breaking through, but breaking through the water fountain is *not* what we had in mind," said Free, with a hearty, earthy chuckle that was enjoyed by all within earshot. Well, except for me...I put down the handbook and picked up *Marijuana Law,* so I wouldn't appear to be eavesdropping.

But eavesdropping was fun, so I headed to the lodge to try and do some more. In there, I hit the jackpot, encountering what seemed to be the head of the visiting massage school consoling two of his despondent students, both of whom were slouching on the couch.

"You're in a place of resistance—stay with it and you'll pop through," said the old man, leaning forward. "You have a wonderful gift. Just *touch* somebody."

That seemed to be getting too intense and I don't think I looked too natural standing in the doorway pretending to be gazing out at the meadow, so I moved on. Out at a far-flung pool I found two commune-dwellers: a fully clothed guy who looked like Kid Rock standing and talking to a tall, tan, butt-naked brunette with slightly pendulous boobs.

"My boyfriend wants to come here," said the woman as she toweled off her inner thighs, "but I don't think he's totally committed to the idea of kitchen work, so he may go to Hawai'i instead."

"Bummer," said Kid Rock, thinking nothing of the sort. Then the two headed down the path.

After they departed, I wandered, passing random people splayed out on the ground here and there, their heads resting on book bags and wadded-up garments. I ignored the signs that read, STAY ON THE PATHS—THE MEADOWS ARE DELICATE, and trudged through a soggy field until it stopped at the edge of a cliff that overlooked the river. There, I spread out a thin towel, got naked, and lay down, letting indigenous plants tickle my butt.

Pretty soon, Julie emerged from her massage and joined me, slogging through the reeds wearing a white robe and a dazed look. "That's the closest thing to a proper beating that I've ever gotten for sixty-five bucks," she said as she collapsed into the grass. Within five minutes, naked hippies cavorting in the river below saw us and ordered us out of the fragile meadow. Luckily for our egos, their admonishing came at the same time as the lunch bell down at the lodge.

At lunch, something weird happened: I loaded up my plate and plunked myself down in an Adirondack chair on the deck, and as I turned around to check on Julie's whereabouts, I saw that she had stopped short, vegetarian vittles and herbal tea in hand, and was quaking something fierce— her face scrunched up, her eyes tightly closed. I wondered for a second if she'd recently developed epilepsy and hadn't mentioned it. Realizing I didn't have any Popsicle sticks to shove in her mouth and keep her from swallowing her tongue, I started to panic.

Julie put her food and tea on the nearest table, and the quaking got worse. All the hemp-covered people began looking at me as if to say, "You're her friend, help her!" But then the fit seemed to subside and she stumbled toward me. As she got close, I saw she had a monstrous grin on her face.

"That's the biggest laughing fit I've had in recent memory. I guess Garde really opened me up," she said before bursting out again and hunching over her food as she spasmed. When Julie was finally able to speak, she explained that what had set her off was a sudden flashback to my description of yesterday's herbal tea as "cinnamon-flavored rag water," and with that, she lost her shit again. Jeez, I couldn't wait for Garde to get his hands on me. No telling what kind of inexplicable seizure I was capable of having at the slightest provocation.

But I guess the hype was too great. When Garde finally set about kneading me something fierce that afternoon, with the smell of essential oils permeating the air, I felt no fireworks. Oh sure, the massage was splendid. Just about all of them are, especially ones that last an hour and a half. But I didn't emerge dropping my food and convulsing over descriptions of tea, dammit all. Guess I'm all blocked up.

Time flew at Breitenbush, and before we knew it, our two days were up and it was time to clean out our cabins and go. Somehow I managed to not attend any exotic classes; I didn't join any drum circles or have any spastic fits. But that was O.K. I'd gotten my money's worth.

As we followed the winding mountain roads back to Portland, all of us were a little sad, but tiny Siena was distraught. She lurched all around in her car seat wailing that she simply had to go back to Breitenbush and stay. She said it just really didn't make any kind of sense to return home.

That child is even wiser than I thought.

Sired in South Florida and seasoned in New Orleans, Suz Redfearn now meanders mostly around Falls Church, Virginia. Redfearn does commentary for public radio and has penned essays and articles for Slate, Salon, The Washington Post, Men's Health, Fit Pregnancy, *and* Health *magazine. Although she has yet to try Watsu, Suz still fantasizes daily about living in a commune with all her closest pals.*

★

When I first moved to Eugene, Oregon, it was the week before my stepsister's wedding and I was immediately swept up in all the preparations. I was in awe of Julia and her hippy-chic, laid back ways. Throughout that week, although she was busy with all the wedding craziness, she took the time to encourage me to trade in my fancy clothes for casual tie-dye, to scrub off my many layers of makeup, and to find out who I really was underneath it all. I had no idea just how many layers I had yet to shed before I'd really fit in.

The night before their wedding, Julia and her fiancé, James, held a party to celebrate their impending nuptials. After arriving at their house, I stepped into their backyard and was shocked to discover a sea of hair, boobs, butts, and what appeared to be "Hippy-Fest 1997." Never in my life had I seen so many naked people gathered in one place. In fact, I don't think I'd ever seen that many naked people in my life—period! There were naked people in the hot tub. There were naked people eating tofu. There were naked people somehow looking into each others eyes and having conversations. There were naked people just standing around and being, well, naked.

I was, in fact, the only person wearing clothes. After the initial shock of dreadlocks and genitals wore off, the next thing I noticed about all of the naked people was how incredibly welcoming and friendly they were to me, a stranger clearly out of her element.

Three margaritas and some good-natured naked peer-pressure later, and I, too, became one of the naked people. Admittedly it was somewhat of a confidence boost to undress while fifty people were clapping and cheering me on, and I was amazed at how accepted I felt having been stripped of my fashionable defenses.

It felt good to be in Oregon, where all the happy naked people were. Where I now happily belonged.

—Betsey Lorenzen, "Surviving the Oregon Trail"

* ✱ *

Honeymoon with Jaws

He'll have her swimming with the fishes, see.

IT WASN'T THAT I LIED TO THE SCUBA GUY. IT WAS more that I stretched the truth out of love for my husband. I've been scuba diving since I was fourteen. But I think the fact that I hadn't actually been diving in the past fifteen years would have been of greater interest to Nick, the dive guy. I didn't mention this fact, and actually dropped a digit off the number on my form so that it read, "Five years since last dive," because I didn't want to drag my more experienced husband through the boring refresher dive that we'd have to do if they knew it had been so long.

Had I not had several cocktails prior to this omission, I might have taken the whole life-and-death scenario thing a bit more seriously. But, alas, we were on our honeymoon, staying at an all-inclusive resort. Drinks flowed like water, and I was almost always thirsty.

The morning of the first dive, I felt nervous and had a tough time enjoying the all-you-can-eat buffet offered each morning of our stay. I scarfed down a couple of tasty crepes with jam and some bacon knowing that I'd need energy in order to act as if I knew what I was doing once we were on the dive boat.

"O.K., so the buoyancy controller thingy," I began, once we were in the van on our way to the dive center. I poked my husband, Dave, in the arm repeatedly to get him to review the details of the equipment that I'd long since forgotten how to use. "How does that work again?" He rolled his eyes at me and assured me that he'd show me how to use mine once they'd actually given me one at the dive shop.

At the shop, we went to the counter to check out our gear. Regulator, check. Buoyancy controller, check. Fins, check. I felt like a pro when I informed the woman behind the counter that I wouldn't need a mask and snorkel since I had brought my own. I flashed her a glimpse of my matching pink snorkel and mask.

"Great," she said, smiling. "How much weight do you need?"

Panic rose in my throat like a bad piece of shellfish. I had no idea. I had forgotten all about the weight belt.

Dave stepped in, "You usually wear about ten pounds, don't you honey?"

"Yes, that's right," I said, pleased that he was supporting me in my deceit.

On the boat, Nick the dive guy greeted us pleasantly, but he must have sensed my confusion as I attempted to screw the regulator onto my tank backwards. He took the regulator from me, and as he put it on my tank, asked, "So, when did you dive last?"

Nervous by now, I answered, "It's been a little while…" I smiled coyly, hoping he wouldn't press. With an eyebrow raised, he turned to address the group.

"So, you all know of course, that this is a shark dive."

The assembled divers all smiled and nodded as my heart struggled to escape through my firmly shut mouth. I turned to Dave, my eyes bulging. How had I missed that this was a shark dive? Did Dave know that this was a shark dive?

"You'll be fine," he whispered. "Just stay calm."

I reminded myself that I'd signed up for all this and continued trying to gear up like an experienced diver who wasn't about to burst into frightened tears. I tried to stifle my fear as I tumbled backward into the water, holding my mask and regulator with one hand, and swam to Dave's side. I tried to take comfort in his confidence, but it wasn't working.

"The BC. How does the button work?" I hissed desperately. He showed me again how to add and remove air from my vest, and we began to descend. I peered below as we sank toward the sixty-foot bottom, taking deep yoga-like breaths and trying to enjoy the sensation of weightlessness. Any Zen-like state of mind that I might have achieved during the descent was immediately erased when I spotted a huge shark circling slowly beneath me, exactly where I would be in a matter of seconds. The shark's shadowy form was turning in tight circles and I began to wonder if I'd read somewhere that sharks can smell fear, like dogs. I pictured his dead dark eyes in my head, and all I could hear was the creepy music that plays as Jaws targets his next unsuspecting victim: *dun-uh, dun-uh, dun-uh....* My crepes and bacon crept back up my throat, and I swallowed hard, not wanting to attract the shark's attention by offering him an appetizer that might leave him eyeing me as a main course.

The shark moved away as we came to rest just above the sandy bottom, and Dive Guy Nick signaled for us to stay there as he moved out ahead of us. I watched as he opened a bag and pulled out a huge bloody fish head. Immediately there were at least fifteen sharks, some of them six feet long, circling around us and taking great interest in the disassembled fish parts being waved at them. They darted in and out of the area where Nick was chumming the water, their weird hinging jaws opening sideways to chomp down on the meaty meal in front of them. One brushed past me, a bit too close for comfort, and I jumped at the feel of his sandpaper skin against my arm. I could have sworn that he shot me a knowing look as he went in for another mouthful of fish parts.

The feeding spectacle did little to calm my jangling nerves, and I struggled with my BC the whole time, trying to keep neutral buoyancy. This effort was largely unsuccessful, and while the other divers floated calmly with their arms and feet crossed serenely as they hung in mid-water, I struggled violently in fits. I kicked to stay off the bottom, stirring up a cloud of silt which swirled in the water around me. I flung my arms around, trying to keep from floating up too high, and yanked constantly at the air tube on the buoyancy controller, letting air out, putting air in. Dave was shooting me hard looks by now, and Dive Guy Nick kept asking if I was O.K. in underwater sign language.

I was great. I was trapped beneath sixty feet of water, surrounded by sharks and clueless as to how to make my vest thing work. I continued to rise and fall as we finally swam forward, leaving the hulking sharks behind, sinister shadows gnawing at their grisly treats.

Once we were moving along, I actually began to enjoy the dive. Fish sporting colors bright enough to embarrass most Vegas showgirls flitted in and out of crevasses in the curving reef. Fan coral waved in the current and schools of

almost-transparent trumpet fish darted between the drifting divers.

Dive Guy Nick signaled me to show him my air gauge,
which I promptly held up for him to see. Through his mask,
I saw his eyes widen a bit and he signaled for me to drop my
regulator and take his spare. I did as he asked, not sure what
was happening. Once I was breathing from his tank instead
of my own, he put an arm around my middle and began
swimming along again with the other divers, as if nothing
was out of the ordinary.

I'm not sure if blushing is evident in sixty feet of water,
but I could feel myself turn bright red as I realized that I'd
breathed through my whole tank in the first half of the dive
and was about to run out of air. Dive Guy Nick, who evidently didn't need to breathe much, was generously sharing
his tank to support my apparently excessive breathing habit
for the rest of the dive.

He was holding me against his chest with one arm, and
swimming slowly along with the rest of the group. Dangling
in his grasp, I felt ridiculous. I was rarely in full body contact
with a man who wasn't my husband, and there was absolutely nothing enticing about my current position. I felt at
once trapped and humiliated. I kept accidentally kicking him
or whacking him with my arms, since I still hadn't mastered
my buoyancy issue.

Dave swam along beside us and signaled me to see if I was
O.K. There aren't many shades of expression that one can use
underwater, so the biting sarcasm that I would have chosen
to respond to this inquiry on the surface wasn't really an option. I made the O.K. sign and continued blushing fiercely.

I dangled below Dive Guy, cursing myself, for what
seemed like an eternity. *Why must I insist on breathing so*

damned much? I wondered. How the hell had I gone through all that air when my husband, who easily had fifty pounds on me and should really need more oxygen, was still doing fine?

After what seemed an eternity, Nick let me go and handed me my own regulator again. He signaled that it was time to head back up.

Back on the boat, I had no idea what to say to Dave or to the guy who had saved me from running out of air at sixty feet. I sheepishly took off my gear and tried to sink into the beach towel I'd brought to dry off with. I leaned my head into Dave's shoulder, hiding and trying to ignore the fact that all the other divers were dying to know what had happened. Dave assured me that they probably assumed that I had grabbed a tank that was

——)——

Swimming up to my man, Fred, I take his hand. I glance up and realization dawns. *This is not Fred. It's the Frenchman.* Oops! I spot my man and wave him over. I scrutinize his face, and recognizing his beard, the only thing distinguishing him from the other men in identical wetsuits, I grasp his hand and swim alongside him. Soon, I notice that he's inspecting me rather closely and I wonder if my gear is faulty. I stare back at him questioningly, then comprehension surfaces. Yikes! I was holding hands with the Swede! I turn around to find the real Fred, his body convulsing with laughter. He extends his hand to me. Giving him the cold shoulder, I swim beside the Spanish gentleman instead, making my cross-cultural, underwater hand-holding adventure complete.

◆

—Anne Merrigan,
"Family Vacation"

already low, and I was happy to let them believe that to be the case. That plan might have worked, except just as we were approaching the dock—and my escape—Dive Guy Nick said, "Wow, you sure sucked through a lot of air! If you come back tomorrow, we'll give you a bigger tank, eh?"

I smiled sheepishly at him and at the other divers on the boat before skulking back to our resort to nurse my fractured pride with an assortment of drinks bearing tiny paper umbrellas. As I slurped down the third or fourth fruity beverage, I pondered the future of our marriage. So far we'd escaped being eaten by sharks and I'd narrowly avoided drowning—and that was just on the honeymoon! Who knew what the years ahead might hold? All I knew right then was that I was about to hold another fruity drink.

Nancy Olds Smay writes about wine, food, and travel for Wine Adventure Magazine *and online at* Wine Sediments. *Despite seemingly ominous beginnings, she and husband Dave have survived almost three full years of marriage without being eaten by beasts.*

SUSAN REINHARDT

* ✱ *

Going to Pot

Looks can be deceiving.

I FIGURED I WAS PRETTY CLOSE TO GOING TO POT WHEN my husband and I took a trip to Cozumel, Mexico, shortly before I turned forty.

Mexicans usually love me. I can always count on these sweet gentlemen to wink or smile or say something flattering, like "*La dama es muy bonita,*" which I think means "very pretty" or maybe it just means I'm wearing a fine bonnet.

I like to flatter myself and pretend they are seeking more than a green card when they follow me around town, getting all out of sorts even if I'm having a puffy-faced, fat-armed, retaining-fluid day.

My husband and I decided we needed a vacation from parenthood and signed up for one of those all-inclusive deals frequented by fatties and alkies, both of which I could qualify as being, depending on the day.

It was supposed to be four nights of romance and adventure away from our kids. It turned into four nights of my husband either sick with a cold or pretending to be, and me enrolling in every activity alone. Everywhere I went I was solo, and not one man, not even a toothless, wrinkled wreck or a staggering alcoholic, hit on me.

This was one of life's biggest wake-up calls, even bigger than when the postal clerk quit blushing when I licked stamps in front of him and he told me to move my business away from his counter.

I mean, here I was, a woman without a man, and not a single Mexican was wanting my affections and thus a chance to fly back to America—land of dreams—with me as his bride and ticket to better wages and a McDonald's in every town. Land of outlet malls and Tommy Hilfiger. Land of Gucci, Vuitton, Pamela, and Britney and other people and possessions those outside our borders find alluring.

This was as bad as walking through a construction site and hearing nary a catcall. This could mean one thing, and one thing only. Someone had gone downhill. Or straight to pot. All that motherly advice about working on my mind had left me with baggy eyes, loose skin, and a goiter stomach. Not to mention the boobs. Let's, for a moment, leave them out of this.

Each day in paradise as my husband flopped across his bed, hacking and snorting phlegm and bemoaning the bad food and concrete mattress, I'd lounge by the pool or beach in my two-piece suits and even the total drunks wouldn't so much as glance. If they did, they quickly glanced elsewhere because at these all-inclusives there are sluts-a-plenty!

One afternoon while my husband lay curled like a scorpion in the bed and snarling about how miserable he was, I decided to take this all-inclusive resort up on its free horseback rides.

The only ones signed up were me and a couple of geeks who looked as if they lived in a town where the sun hasn't come out for months. They were wearing matching "I Love Cozumel" t-shirts and were obviously on their honeymoon, thinking they were about to enjoy a romantic romp through paradise on a former Kentucky Derby winner.

A stout Mexican with a nice smile, tequila breath, and only one missing side tooth introduced himself. I was drinking a beer in a red tumbler that appeared to be the type Pizza Hut uses for its soft drinks. The beer, along with the watered-down liquor, was free, and though I'd later suffer a weeklong bout of E. coli, one doesn't think of such as she sips her diluted offerings and tries to envision the getaway of a lifetime.

The Mexican eyed my tumbler thirstily. "You want me to get you one?" I asked.

"I'm not supposed to drink," he said, darting his eyes toward a counter where his boss was explaining the cost of rental cars. "Go now, yes. *Sí*. Get me one, *por favor.*"

I brought him a draft from the bar and the honeymoon geeks gave me the evil eye. I believe they were Pentecostals, not that there's a thing wrong with them, but they don't like it when tourists and Mexicans fraternize over mind-altering substances poured from a keg and teeming with deadly parasites. They just wanted to get on their horses and pretend they were in a romance novel, the wind on their faces and in the armholes of their "I Love Cozumel" tees.

I, on the other hand, just wanted to drink a bit and escape my nose-blowing, mucousy husband who was probably sweeping the tile floors or making the beds. This is what he enjoys doing in fine hotels. Cleaning and pretending to be deathly ill from germs circulating on the plane rides. He is convinced airplanes are nothing more than petri dishes with wings.

The Mexican downed his beer in two gulps and led us across a dirt road to a patch of scrubby wilderness. He kept eyeing me because I had no mate, a slight buzz, and a snug swimsuit top paired with shorts. It was one of those padded push-up deals, part of a tankini, nothing slutty about it, but I was looking hot in that top. It might have all been an illusion, but it was working. Took me from a saggy B to a full firm D.

We rounded a corner and there they were, a group of swaybacked horses that looked as if they were ten minutes away from an Elmer's conversion. The honeymooners got the horses with both eyes and at least three decent legs. The Mexican winked at me and said, *"Los caballos son bonitos,"* which I later learned meant the horses were pretty. I thought he meant my bonnet-style hat and thus I smiled.

He grabbed a set of tattered reins and handed over a snuffling horse that he called the "*la mula,*" and I knew what he meant. It was a damned mule. A mad-ass mule. I threw a leg over its dipping back and the thing snorted and turned its head and tried to bite me, nostrils flaring and shiny. The honeymooners had already taken off through the brambled path strewn with litter and discarded auto parts, while I tried to get my *mula* to take one step forward.

The Mexican, who had swilled his one beer much too fast, stared at me with wobbly eyes. He tried his best to speak perfect English and get the words out just right.

"I like a mature woman," he said, his eyes going up and down my tankini.

Mature woman! What did he mean by mature woman? He must have been fifty himself, old geezer, and calling me a mature woman.

He trotted off with a wink, trying to catch up with the honeymooners, who were halfway down the path, viewing the scenic trash piles. Burning tires and stiff iguanas left the air redolent of reptilian death and toxic fumes.

I was trying to get my *mula* to move. When I bit its neck and said, "*La mula* is *muy malo* and I'm going to cook your haunch for dinner," the blessed animal stumbled like an old woman with two new hip replacements.

After ten minutes of me trying to get my mule to make some progress, the Mexican leader returned, smelling of belches and lust. He rode his horse next to my mule and grinned.

"I like a mature woman," he said.

"I know. You said that already."

"You have nice breasts."

"No, I don't."

Move, *mula,* move. I started to bite its neck again just to escape this man's conversation and boozy perversions.

"They are beautiful. I like a mature woman's beautiful breasts. Not like señorita Pamela Anderson's soccer-ball breasts. *Muy malo. Comprende?*"

"You wouldn't like these," I said and my mule took off running on its three good legs because I had removed an earring and jabbed the post in its hide. I would apologize later with a nice green apple, but for now, I needed to beat it.

The mule would start and stop, pausing over something nasty and decomposing in its path. I could hear the hoof steps of the Mexican catching up to us. Where were those pale-assed honeymooners? Gosh, this was the ugliest countryside I'd ever seen. I thought when I signed up for this all-inclusive we'd get to ride horses on the beach like in the movies. This was the equivalent of riding through a trail of Dumpsters.

The mule wouldn't budge and I didn't feel right biting or poking it again. The Mexican was on my tail and sighed so heavily I could smell his fetid breath.

"I just want to see one," he said.

I turned toward him. "One what?"

"I like a mature woman. One breast of a mature woman."

"Well, trot on up the path and find one. I'm not mature. You got that? I'm only twenty-eight. I look older because I smoked when I was young and drank too much in college. I had that disease when I was born where you look eighty by the time you are three. Very sad, but I make the best of it."

"You are spirited and I like that in a woman. American women are like my horses. Spirited."

Your horses are two gallops away from glue, I wanted to say, but did not because he was staring a hole through my tankini top with the built-in mega bra.

"Let me see just one. Only one. A mature breast, please."

"I will not. They are ugly. I'm telling you."

"They are so beautiful. And mature."

I searched the ground for a big stick to hit him with, but all I could find were scrubby vines and old plastic cups. I was truly afraid by now. Not another person was in sight.

"Just show me one and I promise I will leave you alone. I promise."

"You will go away? You will run on up the path after the others?"

"*Sí.* Yes."

"Well, all right then."

He began to salivate and sweat. I knew he was in for a shock and the "spirited" American woman in me couldn't wait to see his face when he got a load of the goods this tankini was certainly boosting and plumping.

As he inched his old horse closer to my *mula*, I began to have second thoughts.

"Just one," he begged. "The left one."

"Why the left one?" Oh, why was I even asking?

"It looks bigger. More mature."

Thinking I would be raped if he didn't get his peep show, I lifted the left side of my top and out flopped a long, eel-like tit that fell somewhere near the mule's saddle. His eyes squinted. His mouth curved downward. He nodded, kicked his horse, and fled the scene like the Lone Ranger after a bad guy.

"Hey," I yelled, offended to some degree. "What about the right side? Don't you want to see it? The right one looks a whole lot better!"

> I fought my way into the bathing suit, but as I twanged the shoulder strap into place I gasped in horror...my bosom had disappeared. Eventually I found one bosom cowering under my left armpit. It took a while to find the other. At last I located it flattened beside my seventh rib.
>
> ◆
>
> —Anonymous

By then he was gone. The trip was over. My *mula* eventually made it back, drank some water, and crunched the promised apple I had in my beach bag. I cut my eyes at the Mexican before crossing the road toward the hotel.

He stood there staring, as if he'd been hoodwinked and robbed.

"Things aren't always what they seem," I yelled.

He nodded and turned away. I climbed the stairs to our villa, crawled into bed with my husband, and listened to him sniff and hack until time for my next solo excursion—snorkeling on three reefs in the middle of the ocean.

I dug around for a swimsuit that would hide nothing. I would show my breasts to be what they were, those of a woman who'd lived and loved and nursed two beautiful children. Those of a mature woman.

Susan Reinhardt is a full-time columnist for the Ashville Citizen Times *and a syndicated columnist through Gannet Newspapers. Her work has appeared in publications worldwide such as* London Daily Mirror, Newsday, Chicago Sun, Washington Post, Woman's World, *and many others. She currently makes her home in Ashville, North Carolina with her jazz musician husband and their two children. She is the author of* Not Tonight Honey, Wait Til' I'm a Size Six, *from which this story was excerpted.*

*

After lunch, I headed back to the air-conditioned luxury of the tour bus to await the trip back to Cancun. The driver and I were the only people on the bus. I asked him, "¿*Habla inglés?*" He didn't speak English, so we tried to converse in Spanish. Let me rephrase that, *I* tried. He, on the other hand, had a perfectly good grasp of his native language. We exchanged pleasant hellos, then he, like every other male I'd come across in Mexico thus far, complemented me on my amarillo hair.

I thanked the bus driver, who then said something that I did not understand. Next he did something quite strange; he pulled down the zipper of his pants! I'm not sure if he was trying to show me that the color of his downstairs carpet matched that of his attic, but all I could think of saying was, "¡*No entiendo!*"

That ended the conversation, and the zipper at half-mast was now in its proper place. I never really felt like I was in danger, but to this day, I still wonder which of my Spanglish words he mistook for, "Please undo your pants for me, Señor Bus Driver."

—Louise Schutte, "The Importance of Good Spanglish Skills"

ABBIE KOZOLCHYK

* * *

Take Two Coke Hits and Call Me in the Morning

They gave her the Cusceño Cure.

I'M NO HOTELISTA. I HAVE NEVER CARED ABOUT THE thread count of my sheets (unless, of course, it's zero) nor the fluffiness of my towels nor the provenance of the chocolate on my pillow. I do, however, have my standards, and to apply them, I need only fall spectacularly ill.

What happens next—I would contend—is the true measure of a hotel. And though catching your death on the road isn't widely recommended, anyone who's going to do so should hold out for the Monasterio in Cusco. Granted, you won't get the Cusceño experience of Lonely Planet lore, but in a weird way, you'll get something better.

My introduction to the hotel's death aversion department came last year, courtesy of a decades-long susceptibility to strep. Put a single, lowly Streptococcus bacterium within 500 miles of my throat, and there's no question the twain shall meet. Still, I was totally unprepared for the mutant Peruvian strain; let's call it Inca's Revenge.

Within a day of my arrival, this microbial wonder had laid waste to my throat and—in a thoroughly original twist—

piped searing pain to all my extremities. *Full-body strep.* Who
knew?! The results ranged from a brand new super-mega-
tonsil (a pulsating fusion of the former duo) to hourly guest
appearances by the delirium tremens. Bonus symptoms included an eighth circle of hell-category fever, and the pre-
cipitous loss of even vaguely humanoid speech.

If basic strep reduces me to a needy, whining child, this
newfound Strep-Gone-Wild—coupled with my being alone
thousands of miles from home—made me regress even further. Essentially, and not at all becomingly, I devolved into a
scared, teary-eyed two-year-old who wanted nothing more
than her mommy, but what I got instead was an entire hotel
staff of self-appointed, surrogate mommies (men included),
and a big lesson—you should pardon the treacle—in the
kindness of strangers.

Admittedly, some degree of attentiveness is to be expected at a swank hotel. Still, there's a huge difference between generic, obligatory concern and, say, the yenta-caliber
scolding I got from the housekeeping guy who was horrified to find me in the hall at one point. "What are you doing
out of bed, *niña*?!" he demanded, as he tried to usher me
back to my room. I half expected him to knit me an afghan
on the spot.

Nothing could be more different from the last time I'd
had an immuno-meltdown. I was staying in Brussels, at
posher-than-thou lodgings that shall remain nameless
(though Chez Foque You would be a good choice), where I
was enjoying a strep-flu combo platter with all the fixins
(sweats, shakes, dizziness, aches, exploding tonsils, etc.).
However, there were no hall-patrolling grandparental types
waiting to reproach me for taking substandard care of myself;
rather, there was one bitter housekeeping woman who—de-

spite being assured that she didn't have to clean my room—would periodically peek in, shake her head at me, and mutter endless variations on the "Lazy American" theme as she closed the door. Whether she didn't know I could hear her, or simply didn't care, she kept up the routine to the point that I actually started to feel rude for staying in bed. But I digress...

Back to Cusco and the story at hand. In theory, I was there for a quick stopover en route to the wilds of the Tambopata rainforest, but in reality, my Survivor Peru fantasy was starting to look a lot more like Survivor Walgreens. Forget the two-day dugout canoe trip that stood between me and my appointed jungle outpost; I didn't even know if I could manage the two-minute walk to the neighborhood pharmacy. Clearly, the jaguars, caimans, and howler monkeys would have to wait, and I would have to let them know.

Conveniently, just across the street from the Monasterio sat an office where I could rebook the rest of my trip, and I was on my way over when some seizure-inducing chills struck for the 475th time that day. I knew of only one way to stop them. Despite the 80-degree weather, I pulled on the black wool turtleneck that I had quickly learned to keep on hand, and plastered myself to the most sun-baked patch of rocks I could find in the hotel's central courtyard. Abandoning any pretense of sanity, I lay there shaking, whimpering, and making a general spectacle of myself. And those poor tourists thought they had come to the Monasterio to see its cloisters and colonial art. Ha! Needless to say, I caught the attention of more or less everyone.

Not least, the Guest Services attendants whose job descriptions couldn't possibly have included babysitting a disintegrating thirty-five-year-old, but who nonetheless held a rotating vigil over me. While they brought a steady supply of tea, broth, and faxes (the business center had already begun revising my rainforest itinerary for me), housekeeping was stocking my room with get-well flowers, we're-thinking-of-you bath accoutrements, and cheer-up CDs. At which point I realized that this place had achieved the impossible: out-mommying my own mother, who—even had she known I was sick—would probably have stopped short of music therapy.

Of course, even the warmest of wishes and prettiest of flowers are only so effective against an extremist bacterial uprising. Enter Doctor Valdivia, whom Guest Services had summoned for a house call, or room call, as the case may be. Though clearly a man of science, he turned out to be a bit of a yenta himself. After administering a series of injections, pills, and drops, he sent me off to the bathroom where I was to gargle with a mixture of hot water, salt, and coca leaves (ah, Peru)—first I was to put some socks on, lest the five-second walk across the cold tile floor send me to my grave.

As I began to get better and emerge more regularly from my room, not a single staff member failed to ask how I was, and though I'm usually a below-the-radar kind of girl, I confess to being comforted by the attention. In fact, I felt like I was living out some weird corollary to the *Cheers* theme: Sometimes you want to go where everybody knows not necessarily your name, but perhaps your throat culture results or your approximate body temperature.

All things considered, the Cusco delay wasn't terribly protracted. After a few days in Dr. Valdivia's care, I was cleared for departure. With millions of thank-yous and blown kisses—lest any vestigial, coca-resistant germs infect any-one—I sadly said goodbye.

Yes, my subsequent travels were more enjoyable without a virulent microbial companion, and no, there may not be a booming future in disease-themed tourism. Still, I'm oddly pleased that I got sick at the Monasterio. Though I clearly missed out on some of Peru's greatest hits, I saw something few visitors ever do…the full extent of Cusceño compassion.

Fifteen years into a women's magazine career, many of them spent as a Cosmo *contributor, Abbie Kozolchyk dreams of a day when she's known for something other than her ability to use the word "foxify" in a sentence. To that end, she recently took on the role of contributing travel editor at* Martha Stewart Living's Body + Soul. *For examples of the resulting columns along with her other work visit her at: www.abbiekozolchyk.com.*

. * .

Oh, the Places
She Will Go

*An eccentric family's non-traditional love of travel
gave their daughter a rare edge in geography.*

AS A YOUNG GIRL LIVING AMONG THE CORNFIELDS OF
Indiana, traveling to any state more exotic than Florida clas-
sified you as a "weirdo." In fact, any family crossing the state
line with the intention of doing anything besides skiing,
golfing, or beach combing was stopped for questioning at
the border.

Now don't get me wrong, I love my fellow
Midwesterners, and I'm proud to be a Hoosier. They are a
hard-working, kind, and honest bunch. My "Corn-husking
State Champion" grandfather (yes, he *was* the state champion) farmed his 150 acres of corn and soybeans on his
Kubota tractor until the day he died but sadly, adventurous-
ness is not considered a state trait. Our hometown's most
thrilling event was when the Dairy Queen added a vanilla
swirl to its chocolate ice cream.

Needless to say, Hoosiers are not the worldliest people (at
least those who stay). So it's no wonder that my family fit
into the Bible Belt as smoothly as leather-wearing cattle

ranchers at a PETA convention. While my bow-hunting father practiced squirrel taxidermy in our microwave, my
mother was preoccupied teaching Turkish-Egyptian dance
to a town full of soccer moms whose greatest risks taken in
the past year were wearing V-neck tops to the PTA meetings.

But mostly what set us apart from other families wasn't so
much a singular quality as it was a *choice*. It was *where* we
chose to go for spring break: to *non*-Christian, *non*-English-
speaking, *poor* countries with absolutely *no* Holiday Inns.

While many of my girlfriends were splurging on slinky
bikinis in anticipation of spending spring break on a tranquil
beach somewhere, my mother was busy making appoint-
ments for our medical shots. My parents preferred the
thought of staving off malaria with high doses of mefloquine
and bug repellant to the horrifying image of vacationing
poolside in Disneyland with a giant stuffed Mickey Mouse
at their sides.

Classmates simply didn't know what to think of me. It
was a tradition among the athletes at our high school to give
other students nicknames, often unwanted monikers that we
were helplessly stuck with until graduation. Finding an appropriate name for me, however, proved to be challenging,
especially for the more brawny (i.e. less creative) of the students. During my sophomore year, a popular wrestler settled
on giving me the odd nickname "Ooga Booga" because, not
only did it rhyme, he said proudly, but it effectively captured
the alien-like qualities that my family had come to represent
in our town.

Not surprisingly, talking with my classmates about world
travel was as futile as giving a physics lecture in Esperanto to
a class of deaf students. Yet I did try. During my junior year,
as we prepared for a trip to South Africa during the days of

apartheid, I recall one conversation with a classmate that became typical of many others to follow.

"Why are you going to South Africa?" he asked me. "Don't they kill white people?"

"No," I said with patience. "It's a first-world country. My dad wants to go bow hunting after we drive across the Kalahari by jeep."

He gave me a puzzled look like I'd just told him I brushed my teeth with Crisco and licorice sticks.

"What continent is it on?"

"*Africa.*"

"Which country are you going to?"

"South Africa."

"Where is it in Africa?"

"It's in the *south.* That's why they call it *South* Africa." I was beginning to wonder if he'd ever read a book without pictures in his life.

"Why don't you just go to Florida?" he asked exasperated.

When I returned from our trip I thought the ridicule had ended, but it had only just begun. A few of the high school athletes—I won't say which sport (but they liked to throw a pigskin ball around on the weekends and wear really tight pants and shoulder pads)—switched from calling me "Ooga Booga" to the more enigmatic nickname "Gandhi."

One day after lunch I confronted one of the quarterbacks.

"Why have you guys been calling me 'Gandhi' since I got back from South Africa?" I asked.

"DUH! He's that famous bald guy who starved himself…*that's where he's from.*" He berated me, looking quite pleased. "I would think you would know THAT, *Miss World Traveler*!!"

I didn't have the heart to tell him that although Gandhi had worked in South Africa as a lawyer for seventeen years, he was as much "from" South Africa as Willie Nelson is "from" Papua New Guinea.

After college, I left the beloved Midwest to broaden my horizons. During my first summer out West, I interned as a park ranger at a popular national park in Utah. I soon discovered that, while visitors from countries like Germany and Egypt could identify most major American national parks on a map, their Yankee counterparts had trouble just finding the public restrooms.

One college student from Washington asked me where I was from.

"I'm a Hoosier," I said proudly. "I'm from Indiana."

He looked at me incredulously and leaned in closer, "*Really*? Are you *Hindu*?"

Another park visitor told me she hailed from Kentucky. When asked in which part she lived—the eastern or western side—she looked at me blankly.

"Well, I'm not really sure," she shrugged. "No one's ever asked me that before."

I considered buying her a map and teaching her the directions—north, south, west, east…up, down, left, right—but thought the better of it. If she'd gotten by into adulthood without knowing east from west, she'd certainly find her way back to Kentucky…*eventually*.

In the past eleven years since then, I've settled in California, my parents have split, and I now lay claim to a mortgage and a cat. Things have changed, but one thing remains the same: my family's shared love of travel. Years ago my father married my wicked stepmum on a camel safari in Mongolia, and my single mother backpacked solo through New Zealand and came back with a newfound appreciation for coed bathrooms and the studly, half-clad German back-packers who frequent them. My mother and I now travel together, competing for the most insane trip ideas...whether it's dodging landmines in Cambodia or trekking across the world's highest pass in January with one roll of toilet paper and half a bottle of Diamox.

I thank my parents for our "adventures" which have taught me more about geography, health, and survival than any program on the Discovery Channel ever could have: the tick bite fever I contracted in Africa, the nasty burn on my leg from our boat engine on the Amazon River, or the hippo attack in Botswana that nearly wiped out our family's blood-line once and for all. Like a conscientious daughter, I, too, promise to "enlighten" my own children one day with the same techniques used lovingly on me.

Because one, it's good for them, and two, I'll be damned if they're going to flunk geography.

To this day, I occasionally meet Americans (many of them my own hard-earned friends) who travel and read and who recognize that Uzbekistan is not a type of sausage and that New Mexico is, indeed, a legitimate part of the lower forty-eight. These world savvy men and women give me hope for America's future. Every now and then though, I have conversations that whisk me back to my high school days.

Recently I was complaining to a co-worker how my international trip to England had been botched by a foreign airline.

"I had to call Scotland last night to fix my tickets," I said.

"Oh my God!" she exclaimed, covering her mouth in horror as if I'd just been asked to free climb the Sears Tower. "That's awful! Did they speak English?!"

Working as a travel writer/photographer, musician, and outdoor guide, Rachel S. Thurston continues to share her love of travel with her beloved Mamacita, the subject of the story "Mama Chihuahua: World's Fiercest Travel Partner" in What Color Is Your Jockstrap? *Her work has appeared in the* Los Angeles Times, Santa Barbara Magazine, *and* Food and Home Magazine. *Their most recent trip was to Northern India, where they went camel riding and winter trekking. Check out their adventures on www.rsthurston.com.*

SHARI CAUDRON

* ✳ *

When in Jordan

She'll do anything to fit in.

IT'S AN OVERCAST SPRING AFTERNOON, AND I'M struggling to move a ridiculously awkward backpack-on-wheels through a noisy swirl of families inside Jordan's Queen Alia International Airport. Yes, I'm cranky. Yes, I haven't slept in twenty-four hours. Yes, I want to escape the smoky airport into the fresh air as soon as possible. I glimpse an opening in the crowd, dart toward it, and smack right into a middle-aged Jordanian man.

I freeze. The man turns and looks at my face. Then down at my luggage. Then back at my face. Then slowly, his face cracks into a wide Cheshire-cat grin.

"Welcome to Jordan!" he says.

Huh???

His warmth is not at all what I expected. But then, what *am* I expecting? I've never been to the Middle East, and when I told friends I was going, their reactions ranged from mild concern for my safety to churlish suggestions of what songs I'd like played at my funeral.

But I wasn't worried about my safety. Jordan, though it's

58

located—as they say—between Iraq and a hard place, is like the Switzerland of the Middle East. It's peaceful, and relatively progressive. Instead, what kept me up at night were questions about how to interact with Arab men.

Now, I normally don't worry about how to interact with men. I've been voting lesbertarian since my twenties, which means I haven't found myself in the same polling place as a man for a long time. But here, it's different. Here, I actually have to think about being a woman, and how men might perceive me, and frankly, I'm a little rusty.

The guidebooks warn that Arab men consider Western women to be loose and without morals. (Thank you, Paris Hilton.) They say: Don't look men in the eye. They'll think you want sex. Don't go out with wet hair. They'll think you just had sex. Don't wear tight clothing. Sex. Shorts. Sex. And whatever you do, don't show the nape of your neck. *The nape of my neck?* Indeed. The nape is considered particularly erotic in this part of the world.

There is an anecdote circulating in my mother's circle of friends about a woman who, on arriving in Saudi Arabia, was ordered by a *mutawa* to cover her head. Panicking slightly at such unforeseen bullying, and lacking a headscarf, she promptly lifted the folds of her *abaya* to put it over her head—exposing a pair of unvirtuous legs.

"What are you doing, woman?!!" shouted the *mutawa*.

"I am covering myself; now make up your mind!" The confused expat shouted back.

◆

—Anastasia Kozak,
"My First *Mutawa*"

So how do I apologize to this man I've just bludgeoned without looking him in the eye or showing him my nape—especially since I'm not exactly sure what a nape is?

I do it like any other American: by ignoring him, picking up my luggage, and strutting through the airport as if I own the place.

I spend the first afternoon in Amman, Jordan's lively white limestone city, walking through busy streets lined with dress shops and shoe shops and small stands selling *baglawa*, a thin, flaky pastry layered with pistachios. The traffic is heavy and the smell of baked sugar mingles with hot fumes of exhaust. I pass several clusters of men talking on the sidewalk, sharing hookahs, calling to each other from shop doors. But I see few women, and those I do are covered from scalp to sandal in cloth.

I wander into an open-air fruit-and-vegetable market and pass a young man standing behind a plastic bin of glossy green cucumbers. He's got that cocky attitude of all teenage boys who haven't yet been rejected by enough women. I stand to the side and try to discreetly take a photograph. But he notices me—an obvious Westerner with short sleeves and dyed blondish hair. Encouraged by my interest, he quickly turns around and grabs two shiny round oranges from a crate behind him. He extends the oranges in the air toward me, and when he's certain he's got my attention, squeezes them suggestively.

Suddenly, worries about my neck are replaced by concerns over two decidedly more tender parts of my anatomy.

Leaving the market, I meet up with Adam, another writer on my trip, and together we wend our way through the maze of downtown streets.

A group of four men beckons us from the doorway of a mobile phone shop. I'm hesitant. Even though I've only been here a day, I'm feeling this weird vibrating force field that separates men from women, a force field that separates me from the kind of conversation I would easily have back home. But Adam, an affable everything-is-groovy Southern Californian, has no need for such hesitation. He ambles across the street toward them, and I follow.

The men invite us into their shop, and we're instantly presented with a tray holding two glasses of sweetened Jordanian tea. Adam and I each take one.

"Like the tea?" they ask.

"Very much," we say.

Having exhausted their English vocabulary, the men silently watch us drinking our tea. Then one of them leaves and returns again—this time, carrying a *keffiyah*, the traditional red-and-white Jordanian headscarf. He wraps Adam's head in the scarf in the Jordanian way—tight across his forehead, with a long flap down the back.

Because I'm a woman, I don't get similar treatment. The guidebooks didn't say anything about the protocol involving an Arab man touching a Western woman's head, but I imagine the equation would go something like this: Scarves = head. Head = brain. Brain = thoughts. Thoughts = sex.

But the men must notice how envious I am because after a few moments of quiet deliberation, one of them leaves and returns with another *keffiyah*—this one for me. He unwraps it from a crinkly cellophane package, and I bend forward as he tightens the scarf around my scalp and cinches it into place.

Afterward, I insist that Adam take a photo. I stand between the four men—two on my right, two on my left, and forgetting everything I've read, place my two American arms behind the backs of the two Jordanians next to me. They tense and scoot sideways. Adam takes the photo. In it, the men and I are standing so far apart we look like a string of paper dolls.

Two days later, after a hard afternoon of touring, I decide to rest at the hotel's *hammam*, a Turkish bath. I've never been to a Turkish bath before, but I picture a large green communal pool, women on one side and men on the other.

I don my bathing suit—cover it with a long-sleeve, knee-length white robe —and head to the *hammam*.

There are three men standing just inside the door. I assume I'm on the wrong side.

"Women?" I ask.

They nod.

A shirtless young man with blue-green eyes and a towel around his waist leads me inside the women's locker room where he waits next to me as I hang my robe. He then leads me to a small steam room and points to a white marble bench. I sit there in the humidity and marvel at a country where one cannot make eye contact, but where shirtless men can escort women in bathing suits to their own private baths. Maybe Turkish baths are like some sexual demilitarized zone where the usual customs don't apply. Maybe when the Islamic elders drew up rules concerning the sexes, they generously put in a long list of exceptions. *There'll be no public displays of skin except for inside of Turkish baths, on Tuesdays, or when America has invaded neighboring countries.*

After I've spent several long hot minutes in the steam room, the man with the blue-green eyes returns. But instead of leading me to the glorious pool I've been envisioning, he leads me into a large tiled shower stall and gestures for me to sit inside with my back against the wall.

He then drops his own towel and follows me in.

O.K.

Now I'm getting nervous.

It's not that he's a man and I'm a woman, and we're in a shower together, and I haven't done this kind of thing for a while. It's not that he's a man and I'm a woman, and we're in an Islamic country, and I want to respect the local customs. It's that…well, he's a man and I'm a woman, and I'm kind of shallow and will do anything to fit in.

So I sit against the wall.

He picks up an oversized sponge and starts scrubbing my legs with salt crystals. Then he scrubs each arm. Then he sprays me off with a long silver hose, and I begin to feel like some old Nova he's getting ready to sell.

After I've been rinsed, the man motions for me to turn around. I pivot on my butt to face the wall.

"No, no, no…" he says.

He scoots across the floor toward me, and as he does I accidentally look down and notice his wet black bathing trunks are sucked tightly against his skin. Oh my! *Those* haven't changed much over the years, have they? Embarrassed, I stare back at his face and realize that what he wants is for me to lie on the floor, face down.

So now I'm lying flat on the tile with my right cheek smushed against the hard wet surface. He grabs the left strap of my swimsuit and begins to pull it down over my shoulder. I pull it back up, thinking he just meant to adjust it. But nooooo. He wants to scrub my back, and since I'm wearing one of those middle-aged numbers with the modesty panel to shield my mid-section, he wants the top off.

Of course, taking off a sopping wet bathing suit is not easy under the best of circumstances. This is not the best of circumstances. So what do you do? You tell yourself you're

——— ☽ ———

During my early days in Esfahan, I often found myself ruminating on the fact that it was summer in Iran, and wearing a coat, pants, and scarf outside seemed like something you'd do on a dare, not on a daily basis. Then one day I am struck by an idea—if I wore the manteau without my shirt underneath, I would still technically be in compliance with the rules of *hejab*. When I emerged shirtless from my hotel, I immediately began to imagine that everyone knew I was naked from the waist up. Thanks to my nervousness and dwindling confidence in my ability, should I be caught, to parse the fine semantic difference of being "technically in compliance," this arrangement soon proved to produce as much sweat as the original, so I returned to fully-clothed sweating.

◆

—Andrea Fischer,
"Killing Me Softly"

an adult, and adults, when uncomfortable, can refuse to do things. You can thank him for his time. You can say you forgot to tip the maid this morning so.... *Gosh! Sorry! Really must be going!* You could say these things, but instead, you meekly wriggle out of your top, lay your bare white chest on the tile, and allow him to wash your back.

He soaps. He scrubs. He rinses. He pushes your hair out of the way and gives your shoulders a meager little massage. He then rinses again and turns off the hose, and you pray he won't ask you to turn over.

You hear the steady drip, drip of the faucet. You hear echoey male voices from somewhere else in the *hammam*. You smell the strong herbal smell of the soap. You know he's waiting for you to get up, but you can't.

Instead, you lie there, face down, hair splayed about like some corpse that's washed ashore.

Gently, the man taps your shoulder. Without getting up, you begin to slap the wet floor searching for your suit. You pick it up, hold it to your bare chest, and your composure—such as it is—returns. You tell the man to wait outside while you inelegantly wriggle back into your suit, and wonder why it is you've started talking to yourself in the second person.

That night, in an effort to reintegrate back into my first-person self, I tell my traveling companions about the experience at the *hammam*.

Adam listens quietly to my story. And when I finish, he says, in his everything-is-groovy way, "But that didn't *really* bother you, did it?"

"Nahhhh," I say. "It didn't."

And as I say this, I realize my answer is not entirely a lie. Yes. It bothered me at the time. Yet I've since learned three other people had the exact same experience at the *hammam*, including one woman, although her assigned shower valet was female.

The discomfort is just how it goes with new experiences, experiences in which you don't know what to expect. The discomfort is a sign of boundaries being stretched...of misperceptions crumbling...of growth underway.

And when Adam asks if I'd do it again, my response is both sincere and immediate.

"Not on your life."

Shari Caudron is a Taurus, recovering business journalist, and San Francisco native who traded the California coast for the Rocky Mountains twenty years ago. Ordinary people impress her more than celebrities. She believes happy endings are worth the wait, and she's jealous of Barbie collectors for reasons that are tough to explain here, but you'll understand if you read her latest book, Who Are You People?, *which Entertainment Weekly put on its "Must List!" Caudron's work has also appeared in* The Thong Also Rises, *the* Fourth Genre, The Christian Science Monitor, *and* The Best Women's Travel Writing.

LAURA KATERS

* * *

Once That Gun
Goes Off

Sometimes you get swept up in the crowd.

THE ONLY REALLY BAD LUCK I EXPERIENCED DURING
a solo tromp across the remotely parched, but lovely, continent of Australia, was that one of my running shoes had gone
missing. This bummed me out immensely. After sucking dust
in the Outback for several months, I planned to be in Sydney
for just one day before heading back to the States, and the
only thing I craved, believe it or not, was a long coastal
run—a soothingly simple means of appreciating what the
place had to offer without giving in to the candy-coated
tourism that surrounded every large metropolis. Of course,
with running out, I now found myself with other, less exciting, options: I could take a harbor cruise to Manly Beach;
play tourist and visit a museum; shop away my last five dollars on cheap Australian souvenirs made in China; get drunk.

After moments of contemplating the thick morning sunshine trickling in slivers through the blinds, I decided to start
walking. Sydney was a massive place, with an international
smorgasbord of humans, surely I would find something
exciting and memorable to do.

In my room at The Big, a trendy hostel in the downtown area, I quickly packed up every item I couldn't afford to have someone borrow indefinitely: my camera, journal, and money. I put these into a moderately sized daypack and then stashed my passport and credit card into a personal safe kept at the front desk. Though it was August in Australia, and the tail end of winter, the sun was already intense. I remember that first strike of light well as I walked out the front door. I was a believer in karma, and fate, and that things always fell into place as they should.

My walk should have been simply that, a walk, but as I neared Hyde Park—the central park complete with large shady areas, flower gardens, a giant chessboard, and a towering, stoic water fountain—I spotted huge red banners splashed across every light post. Almost immediately I felt a shift in the air. Something was about to happen.

Then I saw the people.

Hordes of people. There were hundreds, thousands. Looking at the red banners more closely my heart nailed an extra beat: *The 25th Annual City to Surf 14km Race. August 11th.* That was today. A run was taking place today, perhaps the "largest run Sydney ever sees." Stunned, I looked at the amassing crowd. People were coming from everywhere, from behind trees, getting dumped out of slowly moving cars, running down the streets towards some general area which I could only guess was the starting line. Then a voice boomed over a massive speaker system—a low voice, deep, and loaded with enthusiasm.

"RUNNERS! ARE YOU READY?" A loud cheer erupted from the crowd—it sounded like a freight train. Then I heard the opening snap of the gun.

We started to run, or rather, everyone else started moving around me. Astonished and even a bit afraid, I realized that

I'd wandered right into the last wave of runners, easily 15,000 people. I was jostled along as old people in tight running outfits pushed at my back. Then children began to pass me. My fierce sense of competition finally kicked in and I began to run-walk faster. "Maybe just until we get away from the park?" I thought.

After all, I couldn't realistically run the entire race. Fourteen kilometers equates to about nine miles. Even though I considered myself fairly fit, I still hadn't run more than two or three miles at a time in the last six weeks. And, had I known I'd be running in public, I would've dressed more appropriately. I was sporting sandals (yes, sandals), heavy brown sweatpants I scavenged from some throwaway bin, and a ratty t-shirt with a hole in the back. Along with this horrible display of runner attire I was also carrying at least twenty pounds of crap, albeit valuable crap, on my back.

Less than a kilometer into it the whole hoard of us began to head up a huge hill along Williamson Street. The pavement was thick with runners—elbow to elbow a good mile ahead of me and a mile behind. Some were running along the medians or jumping over benches, anything to break away from the suffocating strength of the crowd. Panting, I found myself turning to one of the many runners pushing up against my shoulder.

"Where does this race end up anyway?" I asked an elderly, bearded man (with a body like Popeye). It seemed like a good question. The man gave me a quick once over and a smirk developed in his eyes as he took in my outfit, but then his look turned to one of pity. Australians felt sorry for Americans anyway. Actually, Australians felt sorry for anyone not born in Australia. The place was hard to beat.

"Bondi Beach," he said easily, as if he wasn't running at all, and then he too left me in his dust. I was starting to get some heat on my left heel. A blister would surely finish any chance of reaching the beach assuming, of course, that I was going to keep running.

But just the utterance of those magic words elicited new energy in me. *Bondi Beach.* One of Australia's most famous sand traps. I'd heard plenty of stories. I knew about the buff surfer dudes with the yellow-and-red striped caps, and the shark siren—sounded when someone sees a fin rip through the surface—and the relentless swell of waves. I'd seen pictures of the famous mural wall stretching the length of the beach and strikingly decorated with graffiti art, the scantily clad bodies, the gorgeous water, hot sun, and breathtaking sunsets. If I didn't take advantage of such a random opportunity to see the place I might never have another chance...to look for a shark, build a sand castle, and gaze out at the well-oiled bodies of Bondi.

Three kilometers later I was barefoot in the grass alongside the main street, and running hard. One sandal had flown off during a series of quick maneuvers around a patch of scattered stones, a slow runner, and someone's loose, and very excited, dog. I grabbed the sandal off the ground, flipped off the other, and hit the grass. I was obviously out of place, and obviously American, but I was also gaining what I gathered to be a few fans. One small boy maybe eleven years old took off both of his shoes and joined me on the grass for a few hundred meters. And I wasn't the only tourist running. There were others in jeans and dress shoes. There were men and women in business suits, their Sunday best, with cameras, briefcases, and small children in their arms. Young adrenaline-charged teenage boys roared along for a kilometer or so trying to impress the ladies before getting winded and disappearing. One man ran with wheeled luggage and sported the biggest grin this side of the sun.

Five kilometers along and people were working over-
time, sweating and shining in the sun, shirts unbuttoned all
the way, ties wrapped around their heads. An entire men's
rugby squad ran by in pink underwear. And in between
every obvious "touron" the thousands upon thousands of
numbered runners stormed the streets. *Sixty thousand* runners in all and that number only reflected the ones who had
registered.

The subtle curves and deep blue of Double Bay suddenly
appeared to my left; the impossibly clear water chock full of
very large and luxurious sailboats. Then came Rose Bay, even
clearer and deeper, and as I ran past admiring some of the
distant ships out at sea music began pumping from the storefronts. The morning was still fresh at 9 A.M. and shop owners stood outside with their arms raised in encouragement.
We soaked it up, every one of us. We ran through historic
neighborhoods; neighborhoods with cobblestone sidewalks
and old money; neighborhoods that opened up late and
closed early so that families could still enjoy one another.

The race itself—the fans, the sudden camaraderie—was
completely unexpected and while I was continually thrilled
at the spectacle around me, I was also beginning to struggle.
I wondered how much further I'd be able to make it. Failure,
of some kind, seemed decidedly imminent as I approached
the bottom of what the runners had so appropriately chris-
tened "Heartbreak Hill."

"You've got to be shitting me," I whispered under my
breath, perhaps too loudly.

"Yyyyep," a large, hard-breathing Aussie gasped behind
me, right before he began to walk. I noticed many runners
slowing to a walk for the famous hill. I wasn't sure of the
length or elevation of it and it didn't much matter. What
mattered was that every step hurt and every step seemed to

make me appear farther from the top. I put my head down and tried to think about something else as I fought the twinge of lactic acid coursing through my calves. I simply *couldn't* stop, even though at moments I desperately wished I'd never started. There was some kind of inexplicable union created among people that were suffering together, as if I was bonded with every anguished, grimacing face, even though I would never see any of them again.

Halfway up the hill a woman passed out. The heat of the morning was growing and the pace was picking up. Wary that heat exhaustion was a very real occurrence during any endurance event, I knew that my heavy sweatpants weren't going to cut it. Though it would have been nice to take them off and throw them to the breeze, I decided to forgo any chance of receiving an indecent exposure ticket (I did get one, once, for trying to spell my name in the snow during Oktoberfest in Lacrosse, Wisconsin) and instead asked around the sidelines for a pair of scissors. A few knife swipes later and I had a very homely pair of shorts excitedly flapping in the breeze.

The running became easier as we continued towards Old South Head Road and people began to spread out. "We all want the simple life," one t-shirt stated in front of me and another declared, "Stop starting." Yet another read, "Blood donations do work." Runners could be heard yelling out encouragement to one another, offering a hand, water, snacks to those stopped or slowed. I tossed my ratty t-shirt into a rubbish bin as I passed the 10-kilometer mark, my hot skin relishing the breeze as I continued on in my sports bra.

For the first time in a long time I felt complete and total liberation. The sun pounded down, the streets roared. Horns were blown, race numbers shouted, high school cheerleaders screamed (much to the delight of middle-aged running men), and the classic "Eye of the Tiger" boomed and hit me in the legs like a jackhammer. Waves of energy flushed through the crowd, but we were also beginning to mentally relax, settling into the groove. *This* was why we ran, this mental relaxation, this settling down—not for all of the painful steps that came before.

And then, maybe out of sheer pity (but I like to think not), I received invitations to post-race barbeques, beachside barbeques, next weekend barbeques, two offers to join running groups and even a job offer. Suddenly I wasn't alone but surrounded by a massive community of almost-friends and fools, discovering the intricacies and the streets of a city the most glorious way imaginable.

To set foot in Australia is to experience a land so biologically backwards and environmentally ruthless that one can't help but be surprised to find the people to be the exact opposite. There are an obscene number of gorgeous people in Australia. They are the ones that go out of their way simply because it is in their nature to do so. They somehow affect you; they somehow change your life. They *are* around us, all of the time, but we cannot see them because we are too busy, or too distracted. They open doors, offer umbrellas, buy you lunch because they know you are just a poor backpacker in a foreign land. I never seem to notice them unless I am on my own and very far from home but they are everywhere, and they were stuffing the city streets that day.

Soon enough, and thankfully so, I sensed the end approaching. The last three kilometers of the race were quite thrilling as the road moved closer to the ocean. The crowd and runners grew thick again, almost morphing into a tangle of people with one indistinguishable from the next. Salsa bands played music on rooftops, drum circles pounded out beats, and the storefronts were still loyally adding their own individuality by blaring whatever tunes were handy out onto the sidewalks. The last kilometer leading up to Bondi, the streets were on fire.

And then, finally, in one dramatic moment, I turned a corner and beheld the huge expanse of the Pacific Ocean swallowing up the edges of the land. Bondi Beach was exactly what I thought it would be. Hundreds, soon to be thousands, of people pushed with a last effort of exhaustion towards the tumbling silver line of the tide. I crossed the finish line and followed the others—the bleeding, the limping—straight away to the medic tent. It seemed that whoever wasn't behind us stripped to barely naked and raged into the surf.

"How did you go?" a voice asked from above. I was bent over, busily assessing both feet, briefly fearing that I might never walk again. When I looked up I saw an older woman, her face flushed, a grin dancing across her weathered cheeks. I had to laugh at the orange peels stuck in her teeth. She was already busy peeling another.

"Oh, one hour, fifty," I said. And then, as if to justify the time (though it was still faster than half of the runners), I added, "But I ran barefoot and had my camera in my hand the entire time." I wanted to add the distraction of the ocean as a culprit in slowing my pace as well but she was off before I could say another word. A few minutes later I could still faintly hear her, bent over another runner, "How did you go?"

I accepted the invitation to the beachside barbeque. The couple I befriended during the race (we became friendly after one of them snotted into the wind and it landed on my shorts) guided me over to a huge green tent erected in the sand. Most of the people assembled under it looked delirious, sun burnt, and happy enough to be still. We passed tales and beers around a circle. They were generous with me, with their time, with their food and laughter and in talking to them and reveling in the sun and downright awe of the moment, I realized that maybe I could be gorgeous, too.

The day had been so unexpected in its beauty and inspiration that I even decided to walk back to the hostel, even though I knew I was at least fourteen kilometers from The Big and downtown (wherever downtown was). Back home I used the mountains in Colorado as an external compass to help me figure out where I was, or in which direction I was facing—mountains to the west, plains to the east. But it wasn't that simple on the beach, gazing out at the ocean and knowing that Sydney was a healthy mess of harbors and crooked streets.

I took off in the direction of my best guess—barefoot, bleeding, in a sports bra and torn shorts. I stopped at the first person I saw (who laughed), and then the second, looking for directions that matched. Everyone told me something different while at the same time agreeing that, "It's a bit of a walk." Then I met an elderly woman who admitted she wished she were "young enough and strong enough to make a walk like that again."

I do *more* when I travel with others. More dinners, more planned itineraries. More. But more doesn't necessarily mean better. If I'd been with someone else we would have had a plan for our only day in Sydney. We probably would have hit the manicured trails of the botanical gardens, went to lunch. *Boring.* But I would have, without a doubt, missed the opportunity to run the streets with the masses, alone but at the same time engulfed by the energy of a community that until that moment was mostly foreign to me. I even would have missed out on personally exploring nearly thirty kilometers of the city on foot. The entire day further confirmed the vast amount of potential that lay in the unexpected, and the paradox of traveling alone—it can be the most lonesome, the most terrifying, and sometimes the most exhilarating.

I stayed awake for a while that night, sore as hell and buzzed off cheap boxed wine that a dorm-mate had offered up. I wondered if I would notice the gorgeous people in America when I went back. I wondered what it would feel like to run the City to Surf with proper shoes and a sprig of preparation. I wondered what it would be like to travel somewhere else, a place where women weren't even allowed to run. Would the wind feel as fresh? As safe?

Sometimes I have to laugh at the wondrous fact that some of the simplest things in this life are still free. I can run in any direction, fast or slow, fighting the ache in my bones or giving in to the wind if I want to. Like life, there are the huge hills that we swear at, our hearts beating hard and thick in our chests. Then we coast, always keeping an eye on the horizon, always wondering about the next steep bit, the next scenic turn, the next easy breath. Nothing matters once that gun goes off, the world changes and so do I, but I continue to move, knowing there will always be something new ahead, something curiously unfamiliar, something, or someone, to keep me going.

Laura Katers co-exists with three bikes and one cat and lives in Fort Collins, Colorado, where she is a teacher, and an editor and photographer for Matter Journal. *She enjoys writing about, and exploring, the intricate ways in which all of life is connected.*

BETH E. MARTINSON

⋆ ✳ ⋆

Mommy Nearest

Who says you can't phone home?

MY MOTHER'S VOICE SOUNDS A PLANET AWAY OVER
the European island wire. "Your Auntie Julie asked me if you
have a boyfriend there. Are you dating one of those boys?"

I clasp the phone as if she has the ability to squirm
through it. "No. We're all just friends. Ya know. Platonic. No
nooky."

Even thousands of miles away I can feel the heat in my
mother's eyes. "Beth, that's not funny...." her voice growls
then gets lost in the erratic signal I use for emphasis.

I imagine she has her nightgown on, the powder-blue
one with a basket of Dachshund puppies. These are the
same kind of nightgowns she has consistently bought me
over the years. When I was a freshman in college she bought
me a floor-length flannel nightgown with a monkey strum-
ming a guitar.

My mom slurps tea in my ear. She always drinks it too
hot. In the background my father's watching Mrs. Peel save
the day again in *The Avengers*. He's eating the remains of

Pepperidge Farm apple turnovers and flaky crumbs rest contently on his scruffy double chin.

I smile at the contrast of situations. I'm watching boats move through the Mediterranean Sea. The white sailboats remind me of sea gulls in Cape Cod summer. But we're far from the Massachusetts coast. It's my first day in Calvi on the French island of Corsica, and I couldn't be happier. My mother is wishing me home, trying to understand why her daughter would rather spend a week with three acquaintances—three men—than go home to her family where *she belongs*.

Long after the guys have called their moms, I am still trying to find an excuse to cut the cord. "You have no money to travel," she argues. It is a valid point. I left Italy after my semester abroad to travel with new friends. We were heading to the Cannes Film Festival with a few stops along the way. Nick, Steve, and Mikey had been my classmates, and we all enjoyed traveling and letting the little things slide. They reminded me of what it was like to play with the boys at recess before sex got in the way.

"Beth, you have thirteen dollars in your bank account. What can you buy with that?" What my mother doesn't realize is that being broke is an art form, and I do it exceptionally well. I could live on a euro a day, and somehow still be living it up. "It's O.K. Mom, the boys will pay for everything. I'll pay them in other ways." She gasps. I giggle silently.

"Who are these boys anyways?" She prods me with questions about where I will sleep and whom I will sleep with. "They're strippers," I tease. "They're amazingly built, exquisitely flexible, and tastefully erotic."

My mother, an ADD June Cleaver, imagines the worst. She sees me tied to a wooden bed, three strange, albeit, hairy ape-like men jumping around as if I am their human sacrifice for bananas. She imagines lots of leather, lots of candle wax. I chuckle.

"Beth! Stop being flip."

"I'm just kidding. It's all quite innocent. We schedule orgies for Tuesdays. Besides, you know I have a thing for group sex."

The 1950s guru I call Ma never seems to comprehend that young women and young men can be platonic even if they rest their heads a foot apart. "Bethie, you know there are diseases you can get."

The laughter begins to hurt my jaw bone. "I know Ma. I've been washing off the heroin needles, too." Our conversations always move to either my sex addiction or my drug addiction. She often imagines me in a crack house, the main course of a gang bang.

The myriad supposed suitors I have brought home over the years has been fodder for her Nazi-esque critiques. When I was twelve I brought a boy home to play basketball. While he stood a foot away, my mom called him "scrawny" and "big-headed." "He's no good for you Beth," she said as he began tearing up. We weren't even teenagers yet. I invited him over to kick his ass on the court. The fact that I was a foot taller than him gave me an advantage in basketball, I wasn't thinking about make-out sessions yet.

My mother critiqued every heterosexual male that passed our doors according to her protocol of what my future husband should be. There was the guy who had a wonky eye, the intelligent philosopher she deemed the next Unabomber, the jock with British teeth, and of course, a multitude of gay men whom she wanted me to turn straight. One such friend who loved children, baking, and gossip was proclaimed "a perfect match" for me.

My mother didn't get to meet most men I entertained in college. My idea of dating was less formal, more bar stool. For my mother, having me move away from home was a challenge in keeping tabs on my feminine mystique. Her idea of college was nightly rendezvous and study sessions a la *Debbie Does Dormitory*. She had actually once trotted out the old saying, "Why should they buy the cow when they can get the milk for free?" I still don't like being compared to a bovine.

The trip to Cannes was a secret she couldn't crack…"But you have to sleep in the same room. That would make me feel funny…" she says as I look across the street at the silly boys with whom I am traveling.

Nick hasn't bathed in days and continues to wear the same outfit he left Italy in. His Syracuse t-shirt is growing chest hair. Steve has a ripped tank top that looks like evidence in a domestic violence case. His hair is spiked into five perfect clumps. Mikey jumps in the water like a clucking chicken. This morning I had to tell him his sneakers were on the wrong feet.

My mother sighs to break the silence I create. She's disgruntled that she has to explain to her friends that her only daughter and heir to the domestic throne is off gallivanting with three men in a foreign country. Hardly Paris Hilton, the throne in our three-bedroom suburban home is made up of two dachshunds, about forty Hummels, thirteen teddy bears, my grandmother's dry sink, and baskets hanging from every window frame.

"I just don't understand it Beth. Where are the other girls?" The idea of inviting another female wasn't enticing to me because most of the girls I have traveled with complain too much and pack too many bags (and then complain about carrying their own bags). These guys can go without bathing or changing clothes. It's like having a pack of dogs with me, and I love it. Besides, I grew up with two older brothers and most girls don't like waking up to charlie-horses or getting knocked down in New York-style basketball.

"Ma, why do there have to be other girls? Enough with the inquisition."

"Well what kind of hotels are you staying in? I can't imagine the filthy places you can afford." My dear mother always has a way of spinning things. She just returned from a trip to China to visit my brother who is teaching English. My nervous brother had researched the hotels with Western toilets, found restaurants he thought she would like, and in the end she still cried for the entire week deeming the entire continent barbaric.

"Mom, the hotel is nice. We're in double rooms with showers. It's perfect." In all honesty, the shower was in the middle of the room and the hotel manager—who traipses around in a pink robe lamenting in French monosyllables and sleeps all day—hasn't bothered to put up a shower curtain. We imagine he is awaiting sex reassignment surgery.

Certain details needn't be shared with the woman who popped me out of her womb. Instead, I joke about much worse things in hopes that if she ever does find out about the little discrepancies, they will seem menial in contrast. It has worked well with drug use. Smoking pot in Amsterdam was "experimental curiosity" next to the possibility of having a crack addiction.

"Beth, how can you see the culture if you can't even afford a museum or a restaurant?"

Mikey waves to me from across the road, beckoning me to

hurry along. I consider cutting the wire, hurling the receiver into the ocean, but I can't. I owe her. Steve waves too but then gives me the finger. I feel like a sucker, still attached to my mother via wire umbilicus.

"*M-O-T-H-E-R!* Culture isn't just in food and art. It's everything. I just ate a baguette with a homeless man this afternoon. We split it…" and although I want to go into detail about the experience, I know it will be lost on her. The homeless man had been a poet, something I strive to be. Her idea of poetry is one fish, two fish, red fish, blue fish. Seuss is her Plath. Dickinson, her Waterloo.

"Bethie, I just miss talking to you. I wish you would call me more. It's been more than a week…" my mother's voice trails off. The television is still chatting in the background, the sink is screaming at the dishes, but no human sounds come from her side of the world.

If I were home we would be cleaning the kitchen together. She would do the dishes; I would make love to the Lysol spray. There would be discussions on the latest celebrity gossip, which girls my brothers were dating, the most recent fight between my mom and dad (usually over what they were having for dinner and at what time), and I would share anecdotes of my travels.

For me those discussions were a bridge between our chosen paths. It was getting more difficult to relate to my mother, whose life revolved around family and home. My life was a selfish indulgence of discovery. The idea of getting married and having children was a death sentence I postponed indefinitely.

The smell of club poulet being pressed snaps me out of my reverie. I'm angry that she has forced me to stay on the phone. My friends are waiting, the slight breeze is perfect for sun bathing and I am in the South of France. I want to scream at her. Tell her that my life is worth more and that I will never be mundane. But I know my mother hides her sadness well. This isn't a phone call to annoy me. I look across at the guys—now pushing each other about like toddlers—and hold up my index finger in hopes that I will be done soon.

With a quiet sincerity my mother asks, "When are you coming home?" She sounds older and tired. Finally, I realize why she is keeping me on the phone. She's afraid I might never live at home again. I have one more year of college left, and then I'm officially an adult. Nothing binds me to my New England home. She's worried I might not need her anymore.

"I know you want me to make chicken a la king," she says, noticing I haven't replied. She's pulling out all the stops. First she used the anger, then the guilt, and now the enticing comforts of home. In our family, coming home is rewarded with a special meal. My brother Ryan always chooses fried chicken. My brother Sean gets lobster. For me, it's chicken a la king. Ryan lives in China. Sean lives with his fiancée. There are no more homecomings for them.

As I think about how much time it takes for her to cook the meal—boiling the chicken, preparing the vegetables, mixing the sauce—I realize that being needed is all she craves.

But her role has changed now. It is *she* that needs *me*. "I was thinking of making a chocolate cake with that special frosting you love," she adds.

As time ticks on in France, I begin to feel guilty. In order to prolong the inevitable, I must acquiesce to her demands. It isn't that I am off gallivanting with men in foreign countries; it's that I don't want to be home with her. But I do want to be home, just not yet. She gave me the stability I needed to venture out. She is the reason I can be independent.

"Bethie, did you hear me? About the dessert? Remember the chocolate cake I made at Christmas? I think I'll make that for you."

"Sounds delicious Mom. I gotta go rob some French bakeries for the airfare. I'll be home in about five hundred baguettes."

Food. Love. Currency.

When Beth E. Martinson isn't finding herself in funny situations, she's helping her students learn, grow, and change the world. She writes both nonfiction and poetry and recently completed her Master of Fine Art in Creative Writing at Chatham College in Pittsburgh, Pennsylivania. She has studied writing in Italy, France, and India but is now back in the Boston area where she is a teacher, counselor, writer, and purveyor of the arts.

⁂

My Mama was always full of advice and one of her favorite slices of wisdom was to "always face your fears." I found a way to test that slice one summer in 1971.

I was camping in the deserted back side of Santa Catalina Island, at a little-known cove called Shark Harbor. Apparently drinking way too much the night before, I awoke early with a bladder screaming for relief. Groggily unzipping my tent, I took one step outside and froze in my tracks. Surrounding me were some of the ugliest cattle I had ever seen. Now I am no farmer, but these cows were definitely in need of some cosmetic attention.

Outnumbered by beasts of unknown origin, and decidedly in-timidated, I gingerly retreated into the ridiculously insufficient safety of my flimsy tent. Zipping myself inside I considered my op-tions: pinch my thighs together and employ the "wait them out" approach, or use Mama's "face your fears" plan and pee in front of the herd. My bladder cast its urgency vote and I found myself once again unzipping my tent flap.

I peered through the opening, only to discover a big, wooly-mammoth-of-a-creature staring right back at me. We were face-to-face, eye-to-eye, just inches away from a morning kiss, and then I knew. This wasn't like any cow I'd ever seen—not even a typical bull on a bad hair day could muster such an evil scowl. Not only was I facing my fears; I was facing a BUFFALO! If I had been scared at "ugly cow," now I was petrified at "hideous buffalo."

I gasped, he snorted, and I quickly deemed my need to go outside and pee no longer necessary. Rezipping my tent, I pinched my thighs together and waited for death. A few hours passed and I finally took a full breath. I peeked outside and was happy to discover that the hairy bovines had moved off into the distance. I stepped outside and quickly relieved myself. As I stared off at the motley herd, I suddenly felt quite pleased. I had faced my fears quite literally—and Mama, that's no bull!

—Sharon Ashley, "Mama Knows Best"

* ✱ *

Mama Hanh

Don't be lazy!

FROM WHAT I COULD GATHER, MAMA HANH WAS A mythical hero of the backpacking set. A deranged woman of indeterminate age, she supposedly ran boat tours from the seaside town of Nha Trang to the surrounding islands. But these were no average tours, and Mama Hanh was no average deranged woman of indeterminate age. There were plenty of both to go around in Vietnam, apparently.

What made her and her tours so different was simple. Instead of anchoring her boat serenely in the lagoons off Nha Trang and encouraging her charges to dabble in a bit of snorkelling and a picnic lunch, Mama Hanh turned on the biggest floating party this side of, well, anywhere. Would-be suntanners and on-deck loungers were booted into the water with lifejackets and bottles of wine and forced to join in aquatic skulling competitions against her well-pickled self. And to keep things interesting, she had an underling floating around with handfuls of pre-rolled joints, doling them out generously to whoever drifted his way. It was every backpacker's dream. It was everyone under the age of forty-five's dream. It was too good to be true.

"Follow please, crazy people. You crazy, I very crazy."

There were about thirty of us waiting at the boat launch, and crazy was the last word I'd have used to aptly describe a bunch of people with puffy morning heads and sleep in their eyes. We looked about as manic as a bunch of sloths. Then again, maybe we *were* all suffering a collective lunacy. Who else but the clinically mad would drag themselves out of bed at 7 A.M. to kick off a day with the sole intention of making ourselves as sick as possible by the end of it?

But if we were bordering on certifiable, then Mama Hanh was, by her own admission, completely bonkers. While the crowd of twentysomething travelers was intent on cramming a lifetime of debaucheries into the one boat ride, Mama H had done this every single day for the last twenty years. And from what we'd overheard while waiting to board, she was no slacker, daily challenging the "crazy people" to keep up with her as she sparked joint after joint and poured countless bottles of wine down her gob. For Mama Hanh, running a Booze 'n' Scoob Cruise was not a spectator sport.

Standing no higher than five feet off the ground with a toned, if leathery, body clad in innocuous shorts and white t-shirt, the "infamous" Mama certainly didn't look like a notorious mistress of mayhem. She looked about as disreputable as a peanut butter sandwich. But when she opened her mouth, everything changed. Her voice was grating and shrill, but so were a million other people's. Piss off your own mother enough and you'll know what I mean. It was what she did with that squawk that, depending on your sense of obscenity, either elevated her to the status of innovative linguist or damned her to an eternity in hell.

"You, fucka, move it on my boat," she cawed at nobody in particular, waving the bumbling herds on to a creaking wooden junk. "Go and I fuck you up." She'd obviously gotten her hospitality degree at a very liberal university.

Stunned, excited, and with the natural twinge of bewilderment that comes with being called a "fucka" by your gracious host, we all clambered on board, plopping down on the ubiquitous kiddie chairs and anywhere there was room between massive open eskies of beer. My pal, El, and I annexed a shady spot beneath a rotten-looking awning and sparked up our breakfast fags, bald eagling our giggling peers and muttering the odd exclamation on our surrounds. If memory serves, I believe "Bloody freakshow" was our most popular turn of phrase that morning.

But any conversation, either between El and me or our more sociable crew of English, Australian, and the odd North American backpackers, was made impossible the instant Mama Hanh switched on her megaphone. In much the same way as her name dominated the slate walls of *Apocalypse Now*, her voice drowned out everything else in her presence. Even the circling seagulls swooped down for a listen.

"Hey crazy people!" she screeched. "I say, hey CRAZY PEOPLE!"

"Uh, hey," murmured the crowd, obviously confused as to whether they were on a leaking old boat or in the audience at a Monsters of Rock stadium tour.

"I say, HEY!"

"HEY!" chorused the crowd with slightly more enthusiasm. El and I looked at each other, both thinking the same thing: Uh-oh. If Mama Hanh was trying to get us in the part-aaay mode with a bit of group bonding, she was out of luck when it came to us two. Insta-Camaraderie wasn't our thing. As far as I knew, we didn't have to be forging lifetime bonds with a bunch of strangers just to get wasted. And getting wasted was the point, wasn't it?

Evidently so. "Hey crazy people, I am Mama Hanh. Today, I take you to beautiful place. And I fuck you up." Pause for gasps. "That's right, I fuck you up. You no fuck up, I sorry." Pause for giggles. "I work hard every day to fuck you up, and you work, too. Work at getting fuck up. Don't be lazy."

And there it was. I'd spent my entire life being told by respectable figures of authority to stop being such a layabout and had never listened to a word of it. Now, thanks to the exhortations of a diminutive madwoman, I was going to mend my indolent ways. I was going to work really hard. Now pass that bottle.

As we began drifting out of the small harbor, Mama Hanh continued to fill us in on what awaited us. Snorkeling, stops at a few islands, a seafood feast. Yeah, yeah. "But the best is party," she yelped. "I give you free fuck-up party in the water. Wine, free. Smoking, free. Fuck up, free.

"Now you meet Chris," she squalled into the crackly megaphone, pointing at a thin, bronzed English boy in his mid-twenties who was slouched at the front of the boat, rolling an army of joints. "Chris is crazy like Mama Hanh. You want smoking, you see him." Chris glanced up briefly from his handiwork and smiled victoriously to the crowd, who gawped back at him with a mixture of adoration and seething jealousy. I wondered what kind of TE Score you needed to get a job as a professional spliff roller, and mentally damned my high school guidance counselor. She'd never bothered filling me in on this particular career opportunity.

"You wanna breakfast, I have beer for cheap," Mama continued. Good to hear she was looking after our nutritional needs. "Everything else fuck up, free, but beer you pay. Is good breakfast."

She was either very persuasive or our peers were hardcore pisspots, and El and I were nearly trampled in the stampede to the eskies. There was never a question of getting El to bang down a beer for brekkie, and as much as I liked to consider myself a first-class dipsomaniac, I knew I'd been beaten on the lush front by our cruisemates. It wasn't even eight in the morning and the idea of stomaching food, let alone quaffing warm ale, made me retch. When it came to early-morning repasts, it was nicotine, tar, and carbon monoxide or nothing at all.

"I just hope Mama Hanh doesn't see us," El muttered, taking a swill of the very un-beerlike water she'd brought along. "We'll get in trouble."

I felt my head swim into a strange vortex. In trouble for not getting pissed. If the world ran by Mama Hanh's rules, I'd be a model citizen.

"I'm going to have a drink in a couple of hours," I said, justifying my lamely sober existence. "Aren't you?"

"Course. But till then, let's keep a low profile, in case she finds us and makes us walk the plank or something."

"Or pours a six-pack down our illicitly sober throats."

But Mama Hanh was too busy cavorting with the more dedicated boozehounds to worry about the antisocial abstainers dorking it up over water and Indonesian smokes. While we hunkered down like the original wallflowers, she was holding court before a rapt group of admirers, each of them keen to earn her praise as one of the true "crazy people." They shotgunned beers, blew smoke in each other's mouths and came up with some admittedly creative variations of the word "fuck," but there was no way in hell any of us mortals were ever going to reach Mama Hanh's status of "very crazy." Reeling off dirty jokes in her trademark broken English, she cracked a new beer every thirty seconds and steadfastly refused to share either of the two joints she was smoking. "You wanna smoking, you see Chris. These are mine," she cackled. "Don't be lazy." Sharing and caring weren't her big points, but she made a fine motivational speaker.

By the time the junk anchored in the deep transparent waters off a dazzlingly perfect deserted island, nearly everybody was rat-arsed. Everybody, that was, except El, me, and Mama Hanh. She'd downed a couple of six packs and inhaled about a plantation's worth of grass, but she was completely normal. As normal as a cruise host who called one of her guests "Dickhead fuckboy" could be, anyway.

"O.K. crazy people," she barked into her megaphone. "We here at island now. Now we have fuck-you-up party in water. I bring the bar and you get in the water." She paused and looked around. "Now!"

The Svengali had spoken, and within seconds, the crystal waters of the lagoon were asplash with the bodies of dozens of flailing drunkards. "C'mon!" she cried, pushing the more timid off the bow of the ark. "Go to the best bar in Vietnam! Go! Go!"

We went, we went. Mama Hanh, finally noticing our beerless state, had pegged a couple of cans at us before unceremoniously shoving us overboard. "You're lazy! Lazy!" she yelled to us as we slunk, as much as slinking was possible in two fathoms of seawater, over toward the frolicking group.

Despite our public branding as bone-idle layabouts and the fact that everybody else was going out of their way to avoid us and our possibly communicable uncoolness, we couldn't have been happier. We swam and swilled through swells of clear blue and green water, marveling at the verdant backdrop of the perfect little island, feeling on top of the world. Nothing could bring me down, not our rapidly diminishing social status, not even when one of the life rings Mama Hanh and her crew were tossing into the water sailed out of the sky and thunked me on the head. It was an idyllic morning, and, as it tends to do, beer made it even better.

Not so the wine. "Hey crazy fuckas," Mama Hanh called. "Here comes the bar." With a gigantic splash, a massive floating crate was shoved into the water and, hardly raising a bubble, she jumped in after it. "A bottle for everyone," she gurgled, tugging the bar towards us.

Like seagulls to an old chip, the crazy fuckas descended on the buoyant bar, squabbling over heavy brown bottles of unmarked wine. "O.K., enough for everyone!" Mama cried above the din. "And you compete with me to drink the fastest. All of you." Suddenly, she was bobbing beside El and me. "This means you, fuckas."

El, who couldn't swill a shot of Sambuca without coming up for air, pleaded cirrhosis of the liver, but I'd had enough. Lazy, ay? I'd once downed a pint of Guinness in nine seconds and was occasional boat race champion at university. Besides, I was Australian and I had the luck of Bob Hawke on my side. If he could manage to hold the world's record in yard glass skulling, surely I could do my country proud by coming up trumps in a measly vino-downing comp with a woman half my size. "Gimme that," I said, swiping a bottle from Mama Hanh. "You're going down."

She didn't go down, but if I'd eaten any breakfast that day, I bet it would've come up. That shit wasn't wine, it was swine. It was the rankest, most repugnant and overtly offensive crap I'd ever purposefully poured down my throat, and that's coming from someone who's tried every cask in the Stanley line. But my pride was on the line and I had no choice but to keep on guzzling. And guzzling. And.

"Hey! I win, crazy fucka!"

I tore the bottle away from my lips in disbelief and squinted at Mama Hanh. Bobbing serenely beside me, she held her empty bottle up in triumph and glared disdainfully at mine, still a quarter full. "I win," she said without a slur to be heard. "But you one crazy fucka!"

As she swam away, already screaming for another challenger, I felt the world slide sideways. I was suddenly, irrevocably smashed off my dial and I felt my gorge a'risin'. But it didn't matter. I was now officially a crazy fucka. I've never been so proud.

And I've never been so wrecked. El had taken the wine off me after it looked like I was going to keep trying to swallow it, but once we'd hauled ourselves back on the boat, I'd launched myself immediately at the eskie, grabbing an armful of beers to keep us going. By the time we'd replenished our supply about four times, we'd anchored at yet another island, which looked to my glazed eyes like the identical twin of the first one we'd stopped at. But such trifles didn't bother me, or anyone else on board, by then. All anyone seemed to care about was getting their fiendish hands on some more grog and keeping their joints from going out. With a clarity known only to the mega-hammered, I found that I could see the deep philosophical truth in Mama's "Don't be Lazy" edict. After hours of swilling and smoking, we were dependant on our supply of illicit substances to keep us going. To stop would mean to pass out. And how lazy was that?

The rest of the trip was just haze. There were a couple more islands somewhere along the line, and more skulling contests, all of which I lost dismally. I distinctly remember El throwing a prawn at me during an onboard seafood munch-fest, just before I fell off the boat and had to be retrieved. And I faintly recall seeing Chris, floating in a life ring and handing out joints by the dozen, just before El and I accidentally dive-bombed him and ruined his fistful of merchandise. Thankfully, my memory shut down for good right about then. A lynching wouldn't make for the most joyous of holiday memories.

Tamara Sheward lives with two cats and her long-suffering boyfriend in Sydney, Australia. In addition to stints as a journalist and traveller, she has worked as a toy spider salesman, slumlord's subordinate, Rugby World Cup streaker, children's book illustrator and smut peddler. She is the author of Bad Karma: Confessions of a Reckless Traveller in Southeast Asia, *from which this was excerpted.*

* ✳ *

No Bad Smell

Do you know where your laundry is?

I LIKE TO DO MY OWN LAUNDRY, I JUST DO. IT KEEPS me in control. I would never allow a red sock to fall in with my whites, nor would I shrink my cute cotton *kurtas*. Besides, you can tell a lot about a person from their dirty clothes. Say, for instance, what size they wear, what their personal hygiene habits are like, and as Bill Clinton well knows, even clues to their sexual activities. I, for one, would just as soon keep those kinds of things to myself. Laundry is personal, and God forbid that anyone but me catches a whiff of B.O. or spots a skid-mark in my pile. I wash my own, no exceptions.

My husband, James, and I had been stranded in Seattle for three days on our way to the Philippines wearing the same clothing we'd left Oregon in, and we were about to miss a very important date, my brother-in-law Mike's big fat Filipino wedding. We had become the hapless victims of bad weather and an infuriating series of mechanical problems on an airline I'll simply refer to as Northworst. Those uncontrollable problems coupled with our deeply discounted, screw-you-class tickets had resulted in nearly a week's worth of delays with no possibility for rerouting and *no* access to our luggage.

At the last possible minute, we finally boarded a trans-Pacific flight, and this began nearly thirty-two hours of plane and vehicle travel with no hope of a shower in the interim. In fact, James and I did not make it to Mike's home in the Philippines until eight hours before the wedding ceremony. When we arrived, we smelled worse than a couple of hard-living, hooch-swilling hobos. Our vehicle was immediately swarmed by a hive of curious Filipinos—friends and family of Mike and Jhoy, the happy couple—all of them Clorox clean and decked out in their equally spotless, Sunday best. I was instantly and painfully aware of the contrast between how grubby my hubby and I were compared to the sea of shiny, happy people before us.

There I was in my grit-encrusted, five-days-stale ensemble with a miasma of filth about me. I felt very much like Pig-Pen from the Peanuts comic strip, and I really did belong in the funny pages…funny smelling, that is. What I needed was a good hot shower and a fresh set of knickers, but it looked like I'd have to meet everyone in the Peanuts gallery before I'd get my chance. I glued on my best jet-lagged, travel weary, pseudo smile and spent the next hour being introduced to what felt like the entire town of Bagasbas. When the crisp, clean crowd finally dispersed (possibly due to my odor), I noticed my soon-to-be sister-in-law, Jhoy, standing there eyeing me.

James and I had backpacked around Thailand with Mike and Jhoy a few years earlier, and every morning, before *anything* else could take place, she'd insisted on doing her and Mike's laundry. Jhoy was an ever-vigilant laundress, and

James and I needed some washing…a fact that I am sure she recognized as she sized up the mess that was us. Suddenly—and I swear Jhoy waved her arms like a conjurer causing them to materialize—a laundry basket, some cleaning supplies, and a pod of rather industrious-looking women appeared before me. (Forthwith, these women shall be known as the Pod.)

The Pod twittered something in Tagalog which ended in what might have been "*tsk, tsk*," then motioned for us to follow them to the cottage where we would be housed for the duration of our stay. After being shown around a bit, we expected to be left in privacy, but alone time would prove hard to find in the Philippines. Jhoy, who had very pressing wedding matters to attend to, made a quick remark about laundry to a member of the Pod, shot off some urgent orders in Tagalog, and then took off to attend to her pre-nuptial duties.

James and I were left alone…with the Pod.

"You take shower now? O.K.?" asked a woman with the laundry basket. (We will henceforth call her the Laundry Lady).

"Oh, yes," I replied with delight, "time for shower. You can go. O.K.?" I replied.

She cocked her head to one side and stared at me as I walked to the bathroom and prepared to undress. Sensing another presence in the room I looked over my shoulder. The Laundry Lady had followed me in.

"O.K., you put here," she said politely pointing at the clothes on my back and beckoning towards the basket. "I wash for you," she explained with a smile. "Very bad smell!" she added while wrinkling her nose innocently.

"No thank you," I replied politely. "I can do. I do my own washing, O.K.? You can go. I wash."

She stared at me like I was an idiot.

"I wash for youuuuu," the Laundry Lady tried again this time shaking the basket at me for emphasis.

I shook my head no.

She shook hers yes.

She was a force with which to be reckoned, and the woman showed no signs of backing down. I began to fear that if I didn't drop trou and hand over the offending textiles as requested then she might just start scrubbing them with me still inside.

I was considering taking the shower fully clothed when my husband entered the bathroom and pulled off his t-shirt, casually tossing it into the basket. That was the magic...turning a bit pink, my would-be laundress placed the basket on the floor and stepped backwards out of the bathroom.

"O.K., you put here for washing, I come back," she said as she turned from the room.

With privacy at last, I dropped my soiled skivvies into the waiting basket and hopped into the shower with my hubby. Immediately, I began plotting how I would avoid the embarrassment of someone else washing out my sweaty drawers, and I made the mistake of discussing this with my husband.

"I don't know what you're so worried about," James said while he lathered up. "It's just laundry babe, who cares who does it."

"What about Monica Lewinsky?" I demanded. "Bet she wishes she'd kept her dirty duds to herself."

"Mmmm...that gives me an idea," James crooned. "Tell me you packed a little blue dress?"

"Chill Bill!" I retorted sassily.

After our shower, I gathered our smelly collection of clothes and stuffed them all into a plastic bag. I twisted it closed, tied a knot, and stashed the offensive parcel into the very top of my backpack. Feeling especially proud of my cleverness, I hid the whole thing under the bed.

There. That should keep my shame-pile safe until I have the chance to deal with it in private, I thought.

There was little time left before the wedding and no sooner had I slipped into some fresh clothes when our cottage was once again invaded by a swarm of activity. The Laundry Lady reappeared and was immediately alarmed by the sight of the empty basket. Looking confused, she picked it up and brought it over to me.

"You put washing here!" she insisted holding the basket and peering around the room for some sign of the missing garments.

I looked at her uncomprehendingly and pretended to have no idea what she was talking about. She eyed me warily as I continued to act utterly stupefied. I was about to crack under the pressure when, luckily, I was plucked from this uncomfortable situation by a wedding-frenzied Jhoy and was hustled off to prepare for the ceremony.

The wedding celebrations lasted late into the night and well into the wee hours of the morning. Nearly everyone in the Peanuts gallery had returned to the bride and groom's house after the reception. There they continued the revelry and nourished true Filipino friendships with more San Miguel beers. When I went to bed at 3 A.M., there was still much merry-making coming from the main house, and I assumed that the celebrants would be sleeping off the consequences until noon the next day, giving me the alone time I so craved.

The following morning I awoke at the butt-crack of dawn and looked out the window to assess the post-party scene. To my delight, there were no signs of wakeful life any-where. *Perfect!* I thought to myself with deep satisfaction, *time to do my laundry…in private!*

Without disturbing my sleeping husband, I pulled my backpack out from underneath the bed and removed the plastic bag of cruddy clothes. I untwisted the top and im-mediately my nostrils were bombarded by a bouquet of dirty locker room, wet dog, and road kill. It seemed that the air-tight plastic bag I had cleverly used to keep my dirty clothes separate from my clean ones had, in the tropical heat, ampli-fied what was already a rather rank smell into something that just might gag a maggot.

Holding my nose, I transferred the stinking mess into the laundry basket and set off to eliminate the stench. I got as far as my front porch when I remembered that I had left the much needed laundry detergent sitting inside on the kitchen counter. I set the basket down just outside my door and went back inside to retrieve the soap.

When I returned less than a minute later, the laundry bas-ket was simply gone. Maybe it was more of Jhoy's laundry magic, because I swear it had vanished into thin air. I looked around trying to find a more logical explanation for its dis-appearance but there were no clues to be had. There was neither a soul in sight nor a peep from the house, so what possible scenario could have resulted in my missing laundry? Only the most obvious of course…a rare Asian vulture passed overhead and mistaking my stinky pile of clothes for carrion, flew off with the whole hamper.

"Wake up, we've been robbed!" I hollered at James rudely.

Frustrated and panicky I had returned inside the cottage to inform my husband of the fowl play. He lay there looking at me, seeming impervious to my urgency.

"Huhawhaaa? Your laptop missing or something?" he asked waaay too calmly.

"*No!*" I shouted at him impatiently.

"Lost your passport then?"

"Noooooo, James it's worse, it's...it's...our laundry!" I frantically searched under the bed to see if it had magically returned to my hiding spot of its own accord. "Did *you* take it?" I asked, burning the sleep from his eyes with my glare.

"Calm down sweetie, this isn't an emergency," he said, trying to ply me with reason. "If you left it outside the door then the Laundry Lady probably just picked it up. I'm sure you'll get it back later today and probably all washed and folded to boot. Now please relax, it's early. You want some coffee?"

"Coffee?" I hollered incredulously. "I don't want no stinkin' coffee! I want to know where the heck my laundry went! And actually..." I continued in hopes of rallying some support, "It's *our* laundry, James. Do you know how disgusting *our* laundry is? Do *you* really want some stranger having to smell *your* five-day-old drawers?"

"Better them than me," James replied with a smile.

"Well that's just nifty keen for you Mr. President, but I don't want anyone sniffin' around for stains in my skivvies."

With that I stormed out of the cottage to solve the mystery of the missing basket. Still fuming, I made my way up to the main house where I was amazed and relieved to discover my laundry sitting unattended on the back porch. I looked around quickly. There was not a soul in sight, but my inner senses warned that this was only a temporary condition. Realizing I had little time to react before any more vultures swooped from the sky, I scooped up the basket and made a run for the cottage.

I had gotten as far as the lawn when the Pod returned!

They materialized on the porch, the Laundry Lady amongst them. She looked perturbed and led the march as they came straight for me. I was caught…frozen like a deer in headlights. Outnumbered for sure and with nowhere to run, I knew the gig was up. The Laundry Lady approached me first and immediately attempted to unburden me of the basket.

"I do for youuuuu," she insisted as she grabbed a fistful of wicker.

"I wash my ownnnnnnn," I insisted back.

With neither of us willing to let go of our ends of the basket, I found myself smack dab in the middle of an old-fashioned tug-o-war match. She pulled. I tugged. She gripped. I grunted. We were fully engaged.

Our struggle drew some of the sleepy Peanuts gang from the house, and a small crowd quickly surrounded us. From amongst the gang, my husband appeared with a cup of coffee in hand.

"Found the laundry, eh?" he chuckled as I struggled to defend our wash.

I turned to snarl at him, and in so doing I lost my hold on the wicker. The sudden and rather unanticipated release sent the whole dang basket flying up slow-mo style, up…up…up…it flew into the morning air, scattering stinky, carrion-scented clothes everywhere.

There was a moment of silence, then in an instant, the Pod set to work. They scuttled about gathering up the scattered items.

"Oh my!" one of the Pod uttered as she picked up some sullied socks.

"*Tsk tsk tsk*," clucked another member as she reached for my soiled skirt.

I scrambled to grab James' pit-stained t-shirt when to my horror I spotted my thong underwear lying on the ground halfway between me and the Laundry Lady. She had noticed it as well, and our eyes met in a moment of mutual comprehension. Abandoning the t-shirt, I raced to retrieve the unmentionable. She beat me to it by a tit-hair and scooped up my thong with triumph. She held it tightly to her chest as though she had just won a game of Capture the Flag for her team.

Next, she uncrumpled the lacy trophy and held it high above her head examining it in the sunbeams as though she expected it to refract light and cast rainbows or something. Then without warning another woman from the Pod suddenly snatched the panty and held it to her waist prancing around like some sort of coked-out lingerie model.

"*Sexy! Sexy!*" she squealed with delight as she paraded for the on-lookers.

Emboldened by the laughter coming from the Peanuts gallery, she pulled on my five-days-stale thong over her shorts. She slipped them on backwards and hitched them up to just underneath her breasts which gave her the look of an over eager contestant in training for an Extreme Camel-Toe Contest. (Yes, you guessed it…I shall forevermore call her the Camel.)

"*Sexy! Sexy!*" the Camel laughed out loud.

Luckily for me, the growing audience of males eventually tamed the Camel's tawdry display, and finally my thong was placed back into the laundry basket. James wandered off with the men, who by now thought he was really cool for having such a sexy-panty-wearing wife and all.

Stunned that I had survived the embarrassing episode of Show and Tell, I set about gathering up the rest of my dirty clothes. Finding myself still surrounded by the Pod, I came to that hackneyed realization…if I couldn't beat 'em, well…I'd just have to join 'em.

I relinquished my control of the basket, and after noting that the Laundry Lady looked especially pleased, I reluctantly followed them to the washing area on the back patio. Once situated the women began filling big buckets with water, adding detergent to the mix, and watching the suds foam up with a swirl. Next, the Laundry Lady dumped my pile on the floor, and the Camel began sorting things by color. When she came to my husband's five-day old boxer briefs, the giggles started up again. She seemed fascinated by the… errr…package pocket. After all, James *had* worn them for five consecutive days, and the crotch was, well…stretched out rather suggestively.

"*Ooooooh*," the woman who had modeled my underpants only moments earlier cooed as she pulled James' briefs from the pile. "In Philippines," she said, pointing to the crotch, "…man is like peanut. American man…" she continued, pausing for dramatic flair "…is like HOT DOG!!!" She punched her fist into the crotch-pouch of James undies and wiggled her fingers excitedly. "American man is *hoooot doooog!!!*" she squealed again, this time stretching the vowels for emphasis. "You very lucky!" She giggled. "Hoot doog is *sexy, sexy!*"

I snatched my husband's briefs away from the Camel and plunged them safely into one of the soapy buckets where I began sloshing things about. Noting my lack of finesse, the Laundry Lady immediately cozied up to me and showed me how it was done. She reached into the sudsy mix and pulled out, to my double, maybe even triple bad luck, the notorious thong underwear.

With a sudden flick of her wrist, she had the damn thing turned inside out and lying crotch-up on the patio floor for all to see. Next, she picked up a bar of detergent and began scrubbing at the unmentionable area as though its cleanliness would earn her entry into heaven. Mortified, I watched as she washed, rinsed, and repeated.

When at last she was satisfied, she held the panty in front of her, crotch up and stretched out taut. She looked deep into my frightened eyeballs, and while she maintained perfect corneal contact, the Laundry Lady lifted the crotch of my underwear to just under her pert little nose...and...*inhaled deeply*.

"No bad smell!" she announced with glee. She held the crotch to my nostrils for confirmation.

I had survived the Show and Tell portion of my out-of-control-laundry-nightmare only to graduate on to the Show-and-Smell Hall of Horrors. Still, I had to admit that the Laundry Lady was right. One whiff proved it. My *sexy, sexy* undies harbored *no bad smell*.

Later that day, in a rare moment of solitude, I hung my clean, sniff-tested laundry out to dry and pondered the morning's misadventure. Yes, my dirty laundry had been publicly aired, but had it really been that bad? After all, the Laundry Lady was no Linda Tripp, and the stains she'd spotted on my sundries never led to a national scandal. True, the Camel had detected my husband's *hooot dooooog*, and they both probably knew a thing or two about my hygiene, but it still hadn't made me an outcast. I had become one of the Peanuts gang, and come to think of it, where would Charlie Brown and friends be without good ol' Pig-Pen anyway?

Julia Weiler is a travel writer, editor, and aspiring global nomad. She recently sailed over 1,000 nautical miles during the Baja Ha Ha rally where nearly 185 sailboats in the fleet were treated to the sight of her freshly laundered panties flying in the breeze as they hung to dry in the riggings. She is still recovering. Visit her at www.juliaweiler.com for all the news on her latest misadventures.

. * .

Mi Pulpo
Es Tu Pulpo

She came, she cooked, she conquered.

EVEN THOUGH WE COULDN'T GET THE FOOD CHANNEL, I learned a lot during the four years I lived in a house topped with palm fronds. I learned that boa constrictors really like sausage. I learned that ants—a river of them four feet wide—can sweep through your kitchen and leave it scoured and crumbless. My neighbors just shrugged; of course the ants come out during the rainy season. *Sí, claro*, you should always have a machete handy in case snakes come sniffing around for scraps. Sometimes, things got so bizarre I felt like an extra-terrestrial. And there was no way in that steamy beach town to even phone home.

Fifteen years ago, Tulum was a shy Mexican fishing village, still relatively unscathed from the throngs of sunburned tourists visiting its glitzy northern sister, Cancun, eighty miles away. The town's butcher shop was painted sea blue and advertised its purpose with a pig sporting a poofy chef's hat and clutching a meat cleaver while trotting after a smaller, presumably more succulent, relative. I couldn't even stand to buy stuff there for my dogs; the stench in the tropical heat was so intense. So I learned to do my grocery shopping in the ocean.

Usually I could persuade a sturdy boatman to sell his bounty to me pre-cleaned, scaled, skinned, and filleted. I would pay a little extra to avoid the icky task of transforming a flopping silver creature into something I could sizzle up in a frying pan. And occasionally my fisherman neighbor, Diablo, would offer to share his catch with me, complete with eyes, guts, bones, and tail. I often had little idea of what to do with these presents, and I was really stumped when he pulled an octopus (*pulpo* in Spanish) purple and sliming from the depths of a dripping burlap sack.

"*Para ti,*" he grinned. It looked like something from another planet.

"Oh, thanks," I said, trying to look grateful. Diablo could have sold it in town for a pretty peso to someone who actually wanted it. To refuse his gift would have been insulting. It just wouldn't be neighborly—*mi pulpo es tu pulpo.*

His wife Ceci yanked a second *pulpo* from the bag, and eyed it eagerly, turning it over in her hands, surveying it as I might have done with a flawless cantaloupe.

"*Perfecto,*" she declared, and planted a kiss on Diablo's sunburned cheek. She turned to me, "Do you like *ceviche de pulpo?*"

Ceci had been friendly with me from the start, but she had become suddenly suspicious of my culinary tastes one afternoon when I had impulsively thrust a bunch of freshly harvested basil under her nose. "Isn't it wonderful?" I had gushed. I was thrilled with my little crop, and it was impossible to buy in the area. I learned why when she wriggled up her face in horror. "*Ay,*" she exclaimed as she turned away, "but that's only for the cemetery." I didn't invite her over for a caprese sandwich.

Ceviche is a zippy, refreshing cousin to our boring ketchupy shrimp cocktail, and in Mexico, you make it with all kinds of sea creatures. Including *pulpo*. I did love *ceviche*, but I hadn't even considered the menu, so mesmerized was I, watching Diablo expertly do some rather brutal looking things to the two octopi he had caught. Actually, *ceviche* sounded perfect; cool and simple—precisely the opposite of what I was feeling.

"I'll de-brain it for you, Susi," Diablo said casually.

"*Gracias*," I said in a very small voice.

One more dexterous twist of his knife, and I saw a golf ball-sized gray mass plop to the jungle floor. The next thing I knew, he was passing me my *pulpo*. I reluctantly reached out with both hands, wondering just how to hold on to the slippery gift.

"*No, así*," he said, "hold it here." He had two fingers hooked underneath a flap of skin (the head?) so it wouldn't slither away. I crooked my fingers, too, and a moment later was transporting an octopus across the yard.

Alone in the kitchen, I laid the jelly-like thing in the sink. It didn't even look like an octopus. It was long and limp and a translucent pale pink, like a wet ballerina costume. It definitely did *not* look like the neat little purple rectangle that I had eaten at sushi bars.

Where to begin? Even *The Joy of Cooking*, which

"Once you have sautéed meat, it becomes second nature. It just becomes part of you."

♦

—Julia Child

chronicles how to slaughter a goose, couldn't help me out with this eight-legged wave dweller.

I picked it up again, using my front two fingers, "a la Diablo," and while inspecting it, I noticed something... something awful. In spite of the fact that my neighbor had kindly done me the favor of carving the thing's brain out (thus leaving the handy finger hold) the creature still seemed to be *alive*. I watched with horror as some sort of fluid pulsated under the skin. Disgusted, I flung it back into the sink.

I was just about to race to the beach and hurl the monster back into the sea when Ceci chirped over the wall, "*Oye,* Suzanne, make sure you pound it real good, so it won't get tough when you boil it." Ah, a clue. Pounding. Boiling. I now had a starting place.

First, I thought, I should rinse off the goo. I held it under the cold water, and tried to push the slime down its body, like working the shampoo out of a long braid. But even after two minutes in the rinse cycle the creature still seemed to be producing slime. I kept squeezing, wringing, and rinsing, but the slime level stayed constant. So, I gave up and resigned myself to a slippery meal. Since I didn't know what else to do, I decided it was time to move on to the "boil" part, remembering of course to "pound it real good" first.

I glanced around my sparse kitchen. On the dish rack were two pots, one big knife, and a rusty cheese grater. I didn't have a garlic press, let alone an octopus pounder. I considered my toolbox—a hammer? This seemed just a teensy bit too much like second-degree murder, so instead I opted for that ubiquitous Mexican tool, the Coke bottle. Several weeks past, I had watched, delighted, as a resourceful beach colleague adeptly mashed potatoes with one.

I gripped the bottle firmly by the neck, whacked dinner once, and immediately was showered with goo. Slime flew everywhere. I prayed for a pre-wrapped spinach and feta salad to drop from the sky.

My ego, however, was determined not to let common sense prevail, so I continued savagely tenderizing my eight-legged foe. If there had been any non-rusted metal in my kitchen, I might have seen my reflection: a psycho bringing my weapon down again and again, spattering and staining the walls with each thwack.

I considered asking my neighbors exactly how they managed to create a desirable meal out of such a messy mollusk, but then of course I'd have to admit that:

I was an inept foreigner who definitely did not belong in their beachy paradise, and, like so many Conquistadors before me, I had taken their gracious offering and turned it into something grotesque.

Finally…slimy, disgusted, and decidedly un-hungry, I plunked my *pulpo* into a simmering pot of water. I peered in and half expected the thing to crawl, B-movie like, tentacle over tentacle out of its watery inferno. I clapped a lid over the opening and cranked up the heat.

At last, I had tamed the beast, and I needed a beer. I pulled a chair up near the stove, sipped a cold Bohemia, and watched the pot.

Eventually the part of my brain that controls the higher, less animal, functions was jump-started, and I began to prepare the other ingredients for the octopus *ceviche*. I sliced white onions, squeezed limes, and pulled delicate cilantro leaves from their stems. Handling this vegan portion of the meal made me feel calmer, but I began to sweat when I noticed a purplish foam bubble up from under the pot lid.

——)——

I couldn't believe I was going to voluntarily consume the writhing mass before me. I stuffed it into my mouth and chewed; and chewed, and then chewed some more. I tried to swallow but a tentacle had actually suctioned itself to my tongue. I gagged slightly then used my teeth to pry my food, which had become a mighty opponent, from my panicked taste buds. Mr. Kim, the "cook," and two Korean patrons stared at me expectantly.

"So, is it delicious?" Mr. Kim asked as I finally managed, with what felt like super-human fortitude, to swallow the offensive piece of octopus. I looked around at the sea of crinkled and expectant eyes, and forcing a huge smile exclaimed "Delicious! Yummy! *Mashisayo*! Thank you very much."

♦

—Tara L. M. Lowry,
"Eating My Own Words"

How can you tell when an octopus is "done"— wiggle the drumstick? I lifted off the top, and gingerly looked inside. What was now in the scummy water bore no resemblance to the creature I had started with—this boiled *pulpo* was a hard, curled, knob, half its original size, and reddish purple, just like the rubber chew toy my dogs used to squeak off with. I speared it with a fork and lifted it, dripping, onto my cutting board, where it would suffer the final indignity in its transformation into my supper.

Wielding my weapon, I paused. Do you cut off the tentacles? And what about those alien little suction cups? How should you handle the head? I settled on chopping the whole thing into half-inch pieces, except for the beak (*beak*!?) which I quickly brushed into the garbage. Then, I scooped the whole mess into my waiting bowl of onions, et al. A stir, more salt, a few squirts of lime, and at last I pushed the whole thing gratefully out of sight into the dark of the refrigerator.

The dirty deed done, I surveyed the scene of the crime. Then I scrubbed my hands, the sink, and even the walls, Lady Macbeth-like, in an attempt to remove all traces of my murderous cooking. After I had cleaned up both the kitchen and myself, I cracked open a second beer and felt better.

I strolled out to the backyard and admired my pelt of fresh soft grass successfully taking root over the rocks. I smiled at my prolific vegetable garden teeming with sunburst squash, eggplants, tomatoes, and the slandered basil. I felt less out of place, seeing the ways I had in fact bent the savage jungle to fit my civilized desires for pesto and veggie quiche.

But I knew I wouldn't be able to enjoy the *ceviche*. The very thought of ingesting that multi-tentacled fish was enough to send me scampering to the *farmacia* for Pepto Bismol.

The birds in the tulipan tree started up their evening clatter, the jungle equivalent of the quittin' time bell. My boyfriend Federico showed up, strode through the kitchen, and opened the fridge, reaching in for a Coke. He rolled the icy bottle along his sweaty forehead and paused in the cool of the box, surveying its contents. "Oh hey," he said hungrily, "*ceviche de pulpo. Qúe rico.* I didn't know you could make that."

He served himself a big plateful of *pulpo*, while I puttered around in the garden, sprinkling water on the baby eggplants. "Come here—*amor*, this is *fantástico*," he shouted toward the porch. I walked back inside, and he snaked one arm around my waist, scooping up the purpley chunks with fresh tortilla triangles. "Now *this* is *comida auténtica.*" He heaped the praise on me higher than the *ceviche* topping his chip. "It's so much better than that basil pasta you made last night. You're practically a native Tulumeña, now." He punctuated his enthusiasm with a friendly whack on my ex-pat buns.

I wanted to be able to celebrate my victory over the *pulpo*, to bask in my boyfriend's culinary compliments. But I couldn't take a single bite. I couldn't even stand to watch Federico eat it. I went back outside, climbed into the hammock, and swatted at the mosquitoes who were enjoying their own carnivorous dinner—me.

The brightest of the stars were beginning to come out, as the brief tropical sunset quickly faded to indigo. I could see Venus that evening while I listened to my lover devour the meal I had made. Pity the poor *pulpo*!

Suzanne LaFetra's writing has appeared in the San Francisco Chronicle, The Christian Science Monitor, *many literary magazines, and a dozen anthologies. She lives in Berkeley, California and never, ever fixes octopus for dinner.*

LESLIE BAMFORD

. ✳ .

Death by Vacation

Marriage is not for the faint of heart.

"I FOUND THE PERFECT VACATION," SAYS BOB, WAVING the travel section of the paper, "with scuba diving included."

"I don't know how to scuba dive." I speak slowly and deliberately because of my husband's uncanny ability to tune me out when I am talking to him.

"You could take a course this spring at the pool," he says. "They teach you to use a snorkel and overcome your animal fear of breathing underwater."

"Sounds like drowning to me."

"It's very safe once you're trained. And you can finally get some use out of that wetsuit I bought you."

"It doesn't fit."

"How do you know?"

"Being married to you has made me fat."

"Wetsuits stretch."

"Oh, so you think I'm fat…"

"I didn't say that," he backtracks quickly. "I just think you'd love the things you can see underwater."

I look at Bob more closely. Sure enough, he has a demented look in his eye. The look he always gets just before he tries to kill me on vacation.

The warning signs about Bob's search for adventure were apparent when we were first dating. One night at a trendy Waterloo restaurant, the topic of taking a trip together came up.

"Do you dream about going anywhere special?" I ask Bob, wanting to know more about him.

"Mars."

"Pardon?"

"Mars would be nice. Somewhere no one else has been. Off the beaten track, full of mystery."

"You're kidding, right?"

"You mean you wouldn't go to Mars."

"Definitely not."

"Why not?"

"It's too far. It takes too long. I would miss my friends. The spacesuits would be uncomfortable…"

"But think of the views. I'd go at the drop of a hat."

"So, hypothetically, if I were your partner, you'd go to Mars without me? Be gone for years? Is that what you're saying?" My voice goes up.

"And you would want me to stay here and live a humdrum life when we could go on the adventure of a lifetime? Is that what you're saying?" His voice goes up to match mine.

The waitress comes by, sees the looks on our faces and backs off.

"I just can't believe anyone would turn down the opportunity to go to Mars." Bob's face turns dark, the smile in his eyes fading like a lunar eclipse.

"I don't want to spend the prime of my life going to the bathroom in a space suit," I say, not realizing that this statement would come back to haunt me throughout our relationship. To Bob, it represents my fixation with things practical, my resistance to change, my cold feet compared to his wanderlust. To me, the Mars argument represents the first time I was exposed to Bob's visionary side, to his love of ideas, possible or otherwise, to his penchant for dreaming.

We drive home avoiding eye contact.

In the morning the phone rings.

"This is Bob calling from Mars."

I pause, try to think of something smart to say and can't come up with anything better than, "Hi. How's the view?"

"Not so good. There's all this red dust around. And it's kind of lonely up here. So I'm coming back. Want to do something this afternoon? We could go to the planetarium."

"Sounds more my speed."

We never did make it to the planetarium. But we made it to the altar. Mars is on hold.

My goal, every summer since then, is to stay within my comfort zone on holidays, take my laptop along, get some writing done, and enjoy a little fresh air and pleasant scenery—typical, middle-aged things. Instead, our vacations involve death-defying activities, no matter how blandly they develop from discussions over Australian Chardonnay and Yugoslavian Riesling in the safety of our home in January.

The scuba diving holiday didn't pan out. Bob recognized that it was a losing cause to press for something involving a woman who has gained weight and a rubber suit that no longer fits. So he gave up. Instead, he began to lobby for a sailboat. He dragged me through myriad marinas around the

Great Lakes for several summers, ogling boat after boat, chatting up boat owners, poring over catalogues, surfing boating sites on the internet. The more interested he became, the more my heart sank like a ship in a bad storm. Not that I am afraid of water. In fact, I can swim quite well, but not to shore from the middle of Lake Ontario.

My first experience with sailing was inauspicious, to say the least. Despite the Mars conversation, we were engaged by then and vacationing in Myrtle Beach. I was lying under a beach umbrella feeling safe and secure, when Bob spied an outfit renting catamarans down the shoreline from our hotel.

"Let's rent one of those Hobie Cats this afternoon," says Bob, his blue eyes lighting up like a halogen lamp.

"I'm sure they're too expensive," I reply, hoping to divert him by appealing to his sense of fiscal responsibility.

"To hell with the cost, we're on vacation."

"Do you know how to sail a catamaran?"

"Sailing is sailing—Hobie Cats, Sunfish, boats with fixed hulls—it's no sweat, you'll love it."

"They're probably all booked up."

"Let's go and see."

Before I can think of another objection, he grabs my hand and leads me down the beach.

To my dismay, the catamarans are not all booked. One ratty craft lies on the beach beside a hut with half its thatched roof missing. The boat, if you could call it that, leans at a peculiar angle, one pontoon sticking up like a dog taking a leak.

Bob exchanges money with a tanned beach bum sporting tattoos of ferocious marine life on his upper arms. He says some technical things to Bob about handling the Cat in the strong Atlantic surf. I try to compute the instructions but they sound like a foreign language. All I understand is something about the surf making it difficult to return to shore.

"Are there sharks out there?" I ask.

Instead of answering, the beach bum hands us two soiled orange life jackets. We put them on. Everything is happening too fast. I feel powerless to stop the progress of my own demise.

The beach bum helps Bob drag the Hobie to the edge of the beach. Following directions, I climb onto a trampoline-like mat that is strung with frayed rope between the pontoons. It is dirty and worn. The sail flaps back and forth, swinging dangerously near my head. Before I can voice my final objection, the beach bum and Bob begin running through the surf, one on each side of the craft, propelling me toward the horizon. Waves crash over me as the Hobie bucks and slaps the water. Bob leaps onto the mat beside me, beaming.

The beach bum returns to his hut to smoke whatever he smokes and wait for another suicidal customer.

"Isn't this great," yells Bob above the roar of the waves, as he pulls on some lines coming down from the ragged sail. I stare at him in disbelief as my stomach begins to register the fact that we are no longer on terra firma. Bob appears transported to a divine realm that I never expect to see.

I discover in a hurry that Hobie Cats are extremely uncomfortable. There are no handholds, just the edge of the frame. To stay aboard, I must kneel on all fours on my side of the mat, keeping my head down to avoid decapitation as we come about and catch a gust of wind, careening out to sea.

"Yahoo!" cries Bob.

I look back. The beach bum's hut is no longer visible. I can't believe how quickly we sailed away from shore. All that stands between me and death by sharks or drowning (or both) is the ugly mat against which my nose is plastered.

"Coming about," cries Bob.

The Hobie turns, shudders, comes to an almost complete stop like a dying whale in the swells, as Bob and I scramble around each other, changing sides on the mat so he can remain in position of skipper. I feel nauseated, bile rising in my throat. Just then a strong gust of wind catches the sail and we take off again, screaming across the waves on one pontoon.

"We are leaning over too far," I scream, clinging to the mat. "I am falling out!"

"Just hang onto the edge, you're fine," says Bob as he pulls in the sail to bring the Hobie's pontoon back down. "And it's heeling, not leaning. You're a sailor now. You have to learn the lingo."

"I'm no sailor. Take me back to shore."

"Let's come about one more time. I think I know how to sail this thing now," Bob says.

"What do you mean NOW?" I yell. "You said you've sailed before."

"Not catamarans. The ride is a little rougher than I imagined."

"Jesus, man, this is a fine time to tell me."

"Don't worry, we're fine. Coming about!"

Before I can object, the sail whips over my head and Bob begins to crawl over me. To save myself from being crushed to death by a large man on a scruffy mat, I have no choice but to scuttle to the other side of the Hobie.

Bob turns the boat on a thirty-degree angle to the waves and trims the sail in a new way. The Hobie transforms from a dying whale to a perfectly balanced craft heading for the coast of Africa. My nausea subsides as we stop wallowing in every trough and slapping hard on every wave. The sun begins to dry my swimsuit. I release my death grip on the frame and sit up on the mat, daring to look around.

The expanse of blue water is dotted with whitecaps that shine in the afternoon sun. The beach is a thin brown line behind us. Puffy fair weather clouds line the horizon. It is suddenly very quiet as Bob's gray hair blows in the wind. He turns and smiles at me, his face radiant with joy.

"See how beautiful it is out here?"

I nod, speechless with residual fear and the influx of sensory data.

We sail for a while in silence before coming about again. I have the hang of it now, ducking under Bob at the right time so we wallow less and skim over the waves in the opposite direction without stalling.

I feel myself smiling, despite my fear. "The waves don't look as sinister as they did a few minutes ago," I say to Bob.

"That's because we aren't fighting them anymore. That's what sailing is all about. Being in the groove. One with the rhythm of nature."

We come about again, and begin our turn towards shore like pros.

It is soon apparent, however, that sailing in the same direction as the swells, some of them four feet or more, is a whole new challenge. Each crest hurtles the craft forward at breakneck speed, then we sink into a trough and nearly stall before the next wave shoots us forward. I reclaim my death grip on edge of the trampoline. Nausea returns. I have a sudden urge for my mother to come and save me, which is illogical since she is prone to seasickness, hates boats, and has been dead for five years.

The shoreline seems to be rushing towards us.

"Do you know how to do this?" I yell at Bob.

"Hell, no."

"I thought Shark Man told you how."

"He said something about it."

"What?"

Too late for conversation, we are hurtling towards the beach, high atop a rogue wave the size of a house (or so it seems from my vantage point crouching on the mat). Bob lets out the sail, pulls hard on the rudder and we skim through the shallow water and up onto the beach for a perfect ten-point landing, like he's done it a thousand times.

As I get out of the Hobie, I realize my back is killing me, my legs are shaking and my stomach is still turning.

Shark Man comes down to meet us, takes our life jackets and drags the Hobie unceremoniously up the beach towards the hut.

"Nice landing, bro," he says over his shoulder to Bob.

Bob grins and puts his arm around my shoulders as we start walking along the beach towards the hotel.

"You did great out there. I'm buying you a martini."

"I think some Maalox might go down better."

"That'll pass once you get used to sailing," Bob says.

"I'll never get used to sailing," I reply.

"That Hobie was damn uncomfortable. But you'll love a real sailboat once we buy one."

"I'm never going sailing again," I say, meaning every word.

"Of course you are." He squeezes my elbow to emphasize his words.

Back home from the beach, I contemplate this unwelcome new twist in our relationship and wonder if I should marry Bob. Co-ownership of a boat would be a huge commitment, like sharing a dog or a pony. I weigh the situation, taking into account my pitiful lack of knowledge about boating, my fear of drowning, my desire to stay inside my comfort zone, and the expression of ecstasy on Bob's face when he is out on the open water. I think it is that look that tips the scales. I decide to stay in the relationship.

I have no way of knowing that by marrying Bob, I will eventually learn to sail a thirty-four-foot sailboat. That being with him will force me to overcome my fear of heights and my fear of flying. Not to mention my fear of being lost in the woods, struck by lightning, frozen to death, and eaten by wild beasts. Marriage is not for the faint of heart…especially when you marry someone who wants to go to Mars.

I figure once we're married, I can talk him out of buying a boat.

I have a lot to learn about Bob.

"Here's an ideal vacation," says Bob, a year after we are married. Snow is falling softly outside the window of our living room.

"We could hike the Long Trail from the Canadian border to Massachusetts next summer." He smiles across the coffee table.

"There's no way we could go that far in two weeks." My feet begin to ache just thinking about it.

"We could do one section, then."

"Where would we sleep?" I ask.

"In hostels."

"With sweaty hikers who snore? No thanks."

"We could commune with nature."

"I'd probably catch poison ivy. Or Lyme disease."

"The trail goes over Mount Mansfield, the highest peak in Vermont. That'd be the best part to hike."

"There are mountain lions in Vermont. And bears."

"We could buy a sailboat instead." He looks at me slyly.

Put that way, drowning doesn't sound so bad.

Leslie Bamford enjoyed writing letters, term papers, even exams—anything that someone else was going to read. Being a slow learner, she was forty before she realized this meant she was a writer. Since then, her writing has been recognized locally in literary competitions across multiple genres. She is constantly producing new work, despite her day job and various death-defying activities thought up by husband Bob, with whom she shared ownership of a thirty-four-foot sailboat for several years. To honor her survival in this relationship, she is currently writing a book about life with Bob on land and sea, a fat feline named Blackberry, and her mother's ghost.

* ✱ *

Wax On, Wax Off

It was a rip-off disguised as a bargain.

I'D BEEN AWAY FOR ABOUT THREE MONTHS, AND MY bikini line was in need of some grooming. The do-it-yourself wax strips I'd taken with me really weren't working, and coupled with the unbearable heat of Vietnam they weren't the most sensible item to carry in my backpack.

Walking back to my hotel one day in Saigon a woman approached me in the street and handed me a leaflet. It was for a beauty salon that had just opened offering massages, facials, pedicures, and waxing. Glancing over the price list I thought $5 was a bit of a bargain for a bikini wax, so the following day I went to the salon to check it out. The salon was situated in a decent area, incredibly clean, and had a very Western feel to it. I know it may sound unadventurous, but a Western-looking salon is very important, especially if you're considering having body hair torn from your nether regions. I decided that it looked like a professional place plus the staff was really friendly, so I booked an appointment for the next morning.

When I arrived the following day, a very friendly Vietnamese lady called Garung introduced herself, then ushered me upstairs. I walked into a large room with several beds all separated by billowing muslin curtains and surrounded by vases of fresh flowers. I was shown to one of the beds where Garung asked me to remove my shorts. When I took my shorts off, she looked at me and said, "And your panties."

I've been having waxes for more years than I can count and never in my life have I been asked to remove my knickers; however, being British and trying to absorb the culture of Vietnam, I didn't want to offend Garung by saying "Are you insane! I think you'll find I'll be keeping my pants on." Instead I nervously removed them and lay down on the bed. Garung then returned and asked me to lift my bum.

Again at this stage I probably should have said, "You know what, I think I'll give it a miss this time," but instead I found myself raising my arse in the air while Garung placed newspaper underneath me. Not a paper towel, which you might expect but actual newspaper. It must have been 104 degrees outside, add to that my nervous sweating, and I'm sure you can understand my concerns for laying my damp bottom on a freshly printed newspaper.

It was around this time that I knew it wasn't going to go well. While I lay there with my bottom half exposed, Garung explained that she was waiting for the wax to heat up, and that she'd be ready in a few minutes. I closed my eyes to try to relax myself, but when I opened them again, there were three more Vietnamese ladies in the room. All of whom were looking at me and staring at my unmentionables.

Garung then applied some of the wax on my bikini line and smiled at me. The heat of the wax was unbearable, and I gasped shouting, "It's too hot!"

Garung replied apologetically saying, "Oh, too hot, too hot."

This then caused all of the women surrounding me to start to blow on the waxed area!... So there I was lying bare-arsed on the *Saigon News* with four Vietnamese women blowing on my private parts. I am, according to most who know me, a prude, so this was, as I'm sure you can imagine, a somewhat humiliating experience.

Garung then proceeded to spread more burning hot wax all over me while ripping out hairs, and each time she felt the need to show me what she'd removed. It was as if she was actually surprised it was working. You could say she even gave the impression that perhaps it was the first time she'd tried it. The one thing I couldn't quite get my head around was how intrigued these women were by my front bottom. I mean they all had one, and surely mine couldn't look that different from theirs. Still they seemed pretty fascinated by it and continued to stare.

Eventually, after about half an hour of sweat, pain, and humiliation, it was over. As soon as Garung and the other ladies stepped away from the bed, I leapt up, peeled the newspaper from my bum, pulled on my underwear and shorts, and ran back to the hotel room. I headed straight for the bathroom to see what damage had been done, and discovered that what used to be a neat triangular shape was now red and raw. The few hairs that I clearly wanted removed had been left and instead Garung had ripped off a strip of hair on either side causing somewhat of a striped effect.

I ran in to the bedroom and screamed at my boyfriend, "I've got tram lines. I've been violated, and I've got tram lines."

Over the next few days the blisters calmed down and the odd bit of skin fell off. My once normal looking bikini line now represented that of a failed porn star which I could barely bring myself to look at. In a couple of months I would return home where I hoped that my regular beautician would somehow be able to rectify the damage inflicted upon my once average-looking ladies place.

Jane Hannon is from the Southeast of England but would rather spend her time in Southeast Asia. She loves and protects her back-pack more than anything she has ever owned and dusts it off every couple of years for a few more months away. The only downside she sees to travel is encountering the "try hard" traveler. As Jane likes to say—embracing the culture is what it's all about but for God's sake put some shoes on and stop eating with your hands!

*

I wasn't sure how far to undress, so I left my bra and panties on and sat down on the massage table to wait for Pong. She walked into the room, then handing me a sarong, motioned for me to re-move my bra. As soon as it was off, Pong's face lit up with the bril-liance of a million stars. "Beautiful" she exclaimed, as she ooh-ed and *ahh*-ed at my diminutive breasts. The next thing I knew, she whipped out one of her own tiny titties and reached out to cup one of mine. "Same, same" she uttered in unadulterated pleasure. I must have looked confused because she suddenly grabbed my hand and placed it on her breast, punctuating her point. "Same, same," she cooed again. "Beautiful!" Not wanting to offend my new Thai friend, I smiled and nodded. "Yes, beautiful. Same, same," I concurred. With that out of the way, Pong popped her boob back into its cup and proceeded to give me the best rub-down I've ever had. As I left the massage parlor later that day, I couldn't help but utter, "So long Pong, and thanks for all the mammories."

—Julia Weiler, "Same, Same"

* * *

Cat Fight *Cachapas*

Think twice before you insult the cook.

LATINS ARE REPUTED TO BE A HOT-TEMPERED PEOPLE. Maybe Hollywood created the stereotype with all those frontier cantina brawl scenes. Maybe the Colombians added to it by killing the soccer player who cost them the World Cup one year. Add to the list traditions like bullfighting and movies like *Scarface.*

"It's the chili peppers," Rogelio, the owner of my favorite Mexican restaurant, once explained. "They put hair on your chest and heat in your blood." But the most brutal fight I ever saw in South America involved a very unspicy food called *cachapa* and two unhairy-chested women.

I was spending the night in Cumana, Venezuela. I had checked myself into a bottom-end hotel and headed out to the street for dinner. As luck would have it, there was a *cachapa* stand right outside. *Cachapas* are large, sweet corn pancakes wrapped around a mild, salty white cheese. They are plain, but make a tasty and filling meal.

I ordered one from the lady at the stand. She ladled the bubbling corn mixture from a large vat onto the griddle to fry and began slicing pieces of cheese with a large knife. I was sitting there in happy anticipation of dinner when the *cachapa* lady suddenly raised the cheese knife above her head and hurled it towards the door of my hotel. *"Tu! Puta! Sal de aqui!"* she yelled. Get out of here you whore!

My gaze followed the flight of the cheese machete to see who might be the object of this invective. Crouched in the doorway, with her arms raised as a shield against flying cutlery, was a young woman in a tight white skirt and matching tube top. The black thong underwear showing through the skirt indicated that "*puta*" was more than just an insult, it was probably her profession. She stood up and retorted, in a less-than-masterful display of argumentative rhetoric, "You're the whore!"

My *cachapa* lady, somewhat saggy and wrinkled in a pink teddy bear t-shirt, looked more grandmotherly than whorish. Her response was to grab the next available weapon—a rolling pin—and yell, "How dare you show your face here after you slept with my husband!" It was turning into dinner theater. And I figured it was the wrong point in the plot to point out that my *cachapa* was burning.

The prostitute had recovered enough from the surprise attack to deliver her own verbal onslaught. "You're an old whore and a terrible cook!"

This was the equivalent of insulting someone's mother in all those L.A. gang movies. A sudden tense hush fell over the small crowd of onlookers.

"I'll show you cooking you little slut!" yelled Grandma Cachapa. She grabbed my burned food straight off the grill and pelted the prostitute with chunks of the charred corn patty, reloading with raw ammunition from the vat when that ran out.

Now, it was all fun and games until my dinner got involved.

I was about to say so until the prostitute came running at Granny with the cheese knife in her hand. Three of the men at the food stall sprung into action at this point, figuring blood doesn't do much for the flavor of *cachapas*. There were a few moments of scuffling while two men restrained the combatants, and the third pried loose all the battle weapons.

"For the love of God!" cried the disarmament specialist, wielding the recovered rolling pin and cheese knife exasperatedly. "People are trying to eat in peace!"

Grandma Cachapa took a deep breath and freed one hand to cross herself. The prostitute broke down into sobs. Both were coated with gloppy *cachapa* batter.

"But she attacked me," the prostitute protested tearfully to her captor.

His grip of restraint turned into a consoling embrace. "There, there," he comforted her, picking pieces of my meal out of her hair. "You just shouldn't have said she was a bad cook. That was very disrespectful."

Nobody mentioned the disrespect involved with the prostitute's adultery or more importantly…the mutilation of my dinner-to-be.

The prostitute then picked herself up and went back inside the hotel to clean up for work. Grandma Cachapa fumed in hushed tones with one of the other onlookers. I went to look for a nice boring restaurant with male waiters and dull cutlery.

Lara Naaman is a staff writer at Good Morning Amerca. *She lives in New York City, where she enjoys starting the occasional cat fight of her own these days.*

★

I showed up to the potluck feeling a bit nervous, but I had brought with me a dish that I thought everyone would enjoy: deviled eggs. Everyone commented on how pretty they looked (prettiness is a *big* deal in Paraguay). They also complimented the taste. I started to feel at ease, even though someone commented on my crude way of eating chicken with my hands instead of a knife and fork. I believe she used the Spanish word for "barbaric" to describe it. But they loved the eggs, and I felt happy. Then someone asked me what my hors d'oeuvres were called. I didn't really know how to translate "deviled," so I just picked out the closest words I knew; "devil eggs."

"*Huevos del diablo,*" I said.

Huevos came popping out of mouths and shooting across the table, slick with slimy saliva.

"*¡Mi Dios!*" someone hissed, "*¡Grosera!*"

I couldn't understand why everyone had spit out my delicious little appetizers. What had I done? Later, I recounted the deviled egg incident to my Spanish-speaking friend, Ana. Giggling, she informed me that "huevos del Diablo" did not mean what I had intended it to.

"You see," she explained, "*Huevos* has a double meaning in Spanish, it refers to a certain part of the male genitalia."

It seems that I had inadvertently referred to my hors d'oeuvres as "The Devil's Testicles." Oh well, I thought. At least I won't have to worry about being invited to any more social events!

—Kendra Lachniet, "Lost in Translation"

SUSAN VAN ALLEN

⋆ ✳ ⋆

The Accidental
Tour Guide

Pity the fool…

WHAT WAS IT THAT POSSESSED ME TO TALK TO THAT
American couple sitting across from me on the train from
Florence to Pisa? Usually when I'm traveling alone in Italy,
I love playing "I'm an Italian." I've inherited the right looks
from my immigrant grandparents to blend in, and after years
of traveling here I have the "*la signora*" costume down: fashionable sunglasses, scarf tied just so, and sexy yet functional
footwear.

But as I sat on the train that morning, looking over a *La
Republicca* newspaper I was barely able to understand, I
couldn't help but to blow my cover. It was the guidebook
that seventy-something-year-old couple kept passing back
and forth that did it. They were going over the same pages
I'd read months ago in Los Angeles when I'd first thought
about visiting Pisa—pages that had little to say about the
town except the standard ho-hum about its leaning main attraction. Pages that made one thing clear: Pisa is one of the
world's most famous "tourist quickies."

When it comes to Italian travel, I am not the "quickie" type. The very idea of rushing anywhere in this country gives me hives. Travel for me in Italy means slowing down, getting teased by a tempting alleyway, taking time to explore and discover—not cramming in a visit to a church or monument to go back home and have bragging rights.

I'd planned my Tuscany adventure accordingly. I'd landed in Pisa three weeks ago and spent three indulgent days discovering the town beyond the tower.

For me, Pisa became Jetlagger's Heaven. Unlike other Italian arrival points, where I hit the ground with a list of attractions that must be taken in, in Pisa there's only one obligatory sight. Outside the "tourist quickie" area, I discovered an authentic tranquil medieval town, where I indulged in glorious immersion: long lunches in cozy trattorias, wanderings through the cobblestone city streets as university students glided past me on bikes, and guilt-free afternoon naps from which I'd wake just in time to catch an awesome sunset over the Arno and then leisurely dress for an evening feast.

I'd gone on from Pisa to southern Tuscany to help friends out with an olive harvest and now was feeling the "oh-so-seasoned traveler," wrapping up my trip with a return to my old neighborhood in Pisa, where I'd be welcomed back like family.

I knew I was put on this train at this moment to help this couple out: He a Jack Klugman look-alike, and she small and bird-boned, so I named her Cecily, after one of the Pigeon sisters in the play *The Odd Couple.*

I leaned towards Jack, "Going to Pisa?"

I appreciated his surprised, "You're an American?" look, followed by the obvious, "Yes, going to see the tower."

O.K., I thought, let's pull back on the snooty attitude about those travelers on package deals to Florence who score up points for themselves by hitting attraction after attraction. Yes, there are two ways to travel, my way and the wrong way, but I'm going to let that slide. I am going to become for these two "that mah-velous woman we met on the train to Pisa who turned a day trip into a fah-bulous memory."

"I know some great restaurants you can go to for lunch."

"Oh no, we're just going to climb the tower and get back to Florence."

Perhaps if I'd had my husband at my side to elbow me that "Oh no" meant "Shut up," I wouldn't have launched into my personal *Zagat Guide* of Pisa. I went on about how fantastic the *bisteca* at the Hotel dell'Orologio was, how they must try the swordfish carpaccio at Osteria Cavalieri, and how the places I'd discovered, especially now in truffle season, were such affordable gems compared to what they could get in Florence.

When I stopped to take a breath I saw I'd lost half my audience. Cecily had her nose buried in her paperback, while Jack stayed with me. But his glazed over eyes revealed he was simply playing his part in the deal they'd struck over fifty-plus years of marriage, obeying Cecily's silent signal: "Honey you take care of the nut."

An out-of-body experience was definitely in play (another me out there whispering, "Put a sock in it! They don't care!"), but my compulsion to be a good Samaritan could not be squelched.

I figured switching topics from restaurants to city attractions would win Cecily back. I opened with the treasures of the Borgo Stretto, the arched walkway in the old city, full of cafes and shops. They could wind up on the

Arno, so much more peaceful (less Vespa-infested) than river-side Florence. There they could see the gothic Santa Maria della Spina, the mini-masterpiece church I'd visited on a rainy morning, with water rushing through the mouths of its rooftop gargoyles.

Simultaneously, Jack and I caught Cecily checking her watch, grateful that the arrival time for Pisa was near and they'd soon be rid of me.

Fine, I thought turning away to gather up my things. I won't warn you what you'll get when you visit the world's most popular architectural mistake. You wanna know what it looks like these days? The leaning two-bottom tiers of scaffolding, that's what. The Campo dei Miracoli—that "glorious grassy piazza that surrounds the Tower, Baptistery, Duomo, and Camposanto" you've just read about? It's framed by a clunky metal fence thanks to 9/11. All that's glorious surrounding it are the handsome guards who make the throngs of tourists toting camcorders milling about it look all the more dreadful.

Pan out further to the schlocky souvenir stands with shelves of every ridiculous incarnation of the leaning thing you can imagine and there's a memory for you. Go ahead, climb the tower like I did. Circle up 300 steps with a family from Colorado, complete with two elementary school-aged boys—their yelps echoing along with the reconstruction whines of metal drills against stone, their mother *rat-tat-tatting* in my ear about the Mommy-lit novel she'd written, and Dad bringing up the rear cursing that the batteries in his camera were wearing down. Add that to your list of "been there done that."

The train pulled into the Pisa station. As I wheeled my suitcase towards the exit, I nodded a farewell to Jack and

Cecily. That's when I caught a look on their faces that stopped me in my tracks. It was unmistakably a look of pity. They were feeling sorry for the lone female who couldn't shut up. *Wait a minute! I started my whole conversation with you two out of pity and now...you're pitying me?*

I had to blast out cheerfulness to set them straight: "We could share a cab. My hotel's on the way to the tower."

Cecily clutched her purse and Jack gave me a stern, "No, no, that won't be necessary," as they headed to an opposite exit.

When I saw them two parties away in the taxi line, I couldn't resist going for a final mah-velous impression, with an enthusiastic *"Ciao, buon viaggio!"* Cecily turned away and Jack's panicked wave read more like, "Go away!" than *"Arrivederci."* I'd transformed in their eyes from pesky know-it-all traveler to pitiful blabbering solo woman to someone they were imagining they would read about in a magazine "Warning Section" back home: *Beware the lone woman who appears helpful. She'll offer great restaurant advice, but she's actually in cahoots with a local cab driver. She'll get you in a taxi and then they'll both rob you blind!*

As I rode to my hotel, I played the train scene back in my head. Yes, that fortysomething-year-old solo woman traveler overflowing with enthusiasm, may have appeared a bit intrusive to those seeking a "tourist quickie."

I remembered all those warnings caring friends had sent me about solo woman travelers. I'd only glanced over them: "Carry a money belt, pay the extra price to stay at a safe hotel, avoid dark alleys..." But what those warnings did not include was: Be aware that at times...such as when one has been three weeks picking olives with natives and struggling with her pidgin Italian and sign language, the opportunity to form coherent sentences that will be understood by others and share your adventures may be misinterpreted as intrusive, pathetic babbling and you shall receive the backlash. That would be fellow travelers regarding you as pathetic…or worse.

Ouch. I calmed myself with a few hours of shopping in the markets for souvenirs to bring back to LA: *vin santo*, pecorino cheeses, and *cantucci*. I treated myself to a lunch of pasta with Chianti. Then instead of heading for the traditional nap, I realized I had to get a souvenir for my nephew and only something tower-related would do. So I headed back to the Campo dei Miracoli.

After picking up an appropriate hideous pennant, I curved toward the tower for a final look. There I saw Jack, frantically waving for a cab, all of which at lunchtime were lined up driverless. I knew he saw me by the look of horror on his face. And there was Cecily two steps behind him, equally horrified. My appearance was the perfect end to their movie: like Glenn Close rising from the bathtub in *Fatal Attraction*.

I could have told Jack the drivers would be back in fifteen minutes after they'd finished their pasta, but instead I went along with his "we don't see each other" game. I turned back to the old city, readjusted my scarf so it was "just so" and got back to playing my safe traditional "I'm an Italian," nodding a *buona sera* to a woman passing by.

Susan Van Allen is a Los Angeles-based writer who has written for National Public Radio's "Savvy Traveler" and "Marketplace," CNN.com, newspapers, magazines, web sites, and the television show Everybody Loves Raymond. *She travels to Italy as often as possible, to blend in with the natives, visit relatives, eat and drink well, bike through the countryside, wander through museums, and enjoy the flirtations of those handsome Italian men.*

. ✷ .

Dear Diary

Get ready to hit the road.

FEBRUARY 28, 2003

Dear Diary,

My thirty-five-city *Here and Now* stand-up tour starts in a week. I've decided that I should keep a journal to chronicle my adventures on the road. I tried to keep one on my last tour but I didn't have the discipline. Not this time. This time Diary, I vow to write in you every day, even though I have a huge problem finishing things I start. It seems to me that

March 3, 2003

Dear Diary,

I've been working out my act at a few clubs around Los Angeles. Last night went great. Of course, at this stage of the process I haven't memorized anything, so I'm still reading off notes I've written all over my hands. The audience didn't seem to mind. Even though I started out every joke with, "Hands sure are funny, aren't they?" while staring intently at my palms...

March 7, 2003

Dear Diary,

I leave in two days, so I guess it's time for me to think about what I'm going to bring. When I'm on tour I usually travel with about fifteen steamer trunks. The hardest part is figuring out what I'll wear for each show. Should I wear a pair of pants? Or should I wear pants instead? I weigh the options. Pants? Or pants? Then I realize I'm usually most comfortable onstage in pants. Still, bringing along some pants is probably a good idea. Just in case I change my mind…

March 8, 2003

Dear Diary,

I'm going to stop writing "Dear Diary" at the beginning of each entry. There's no need for it. I'm just writing to myself. I suppose I could begin with "Dear Ellen," but then it would be as if I've got a second personality with the same name and personality as my main personality. Anyway, I spent most of my day working on my act. Getting my material just right for an audience takes a lot of serious preparation, so I practiced my routine in front of my cats. They always have pages and pages of notes for me. The critiques usually focus on why there aren't more jokes about cats in my act. Why don't I have a "Phone Call to a Cat" joke or a "What if Gloria Estefan Was a Cat" bit? I try to explain to them that my audience does not usually consist of cats, but they feel that I'm limiting myself. Maybe they're right. You know what they say about a cat's intuition…or is it the nine lives of a good woman?

I've also decided to learn about each city I'm visiting on my tour. It's so important to connect with the crowds at my shows. When I take the stage I want to say more than just: "It's great to be here in (insert your city here)!" With the intensive research I've been doing, I'll be able to open with: "Hello, Kansas City! Did you know that your annual relative humidity is 60 percent? You guys ROCK!!"

March 9—Luther Burbank Center, Santa Rosa, Calif

Well, I've finally hit the road. I just finished up two shows in Santa Rosa, California. Both performances were sold out! I was so excited when I heard. I was afraid I was going to have to take a bullhorn to the mall and give the tickets away. Since I didn't have to, I had more time to shower and change before the show.

Speaking of which, my act is really starting to take shape. The best part was that the audience was definitely laughing with me and not at me. Like the time I performed with my oxford shirt on backwards by mistake. You'd think someone would have told me before I went on.

The staff at Luther Burbank Center was so accommodating. The theater had a very nice green room. "Green room" is a fancy showbiz term for a backstage waiting area. It's not actually green. But no one dares ever mention that. Not if they want to keep their jobs. The room was appointed with my few simple requirements: just a big bathroom, a comfy couch, and a kiln, in case I want to calm my pre-show jitters by fashioning an urn.

March 11—Capitol Theatre, Yakima, Wash.

I was a little nervous about performing in Yakima. It's a pretty small town. Very quaint. I didn't know if they'd accept a city girl like me, coming in with all my fancy city ways— my highlighted hair, my constant use of the word "barista," my subway tokens. I couldn't have been more wrong. The people of Yakima ("Yakimites," as I now call them) were so warm and kind and polite. And they love to laugh. I'm now putting Yakima on my list of top ten favorite cities along with Paris and Rome.

March 14—Kansas City, Mo.

Arrived in Kansas City late last night. Checked in to my hotel under my usual alias, "Nelle Sereneged," but the hotel clerk wasn't fooled by my little charade. He said, "But Miss DeGeneres, that's just your name backwards." With my cover blown, I hastily checked in as Gwyneth Paltrow, only to notice Gwyneth waiting to check in right behind me. What are the odds?!

March 18—Grand Junction and Colorado Springs, Colo.

I loved performing at Kansas City's Midland Theater, a beautiful old building built in 1927. Sammy Davis Jr. and Dolly Parton have played there, so I guess it was only a matter of time before I did. As a performer, I've always felt I was the perfect mixture of those two, with a dash of Carol Channing for zest. Then it was on to Grand Junction, Colorado, and Colorado Springs. Both shows were a delight.

Have I mentioned my opening act? Karen Kilgariff is the head writer for my new talk show and she's been traveling with me for the entire tour. She's been doing an amazing job warming up the crowds. Having a warm-up act is kind of like having your own personal food taster. Karen bravely goes out there to see if the crowd is good; that is, if they "taste" good to her. Some audiences of course are an acquired taste, but if Karen thinks the audience is "poison" (meaning sleepy and unresponsive), I don't go on. Instead, I am whisked out the back door to the safety of a cozy neighborhood bistro...

March 19—Colorado to Seattle

I'm writing this as we drive through the frozen tundra of Colorado toward an airport that might be open so I can get to Seattle for a 7:30 show. There was a huge snowstorm; most of the roads are closed. We've been driving in the storm for two hours and have a couple more to go. We're all hungry, but there is not one store or restaurant open. In a desperate attempt to eat, I tried ordering room service, but realized that our hotel would have to airlift the food to our car.

The Denver show was canceled because no one could get to the theater in the blizzard. I'll be back in Denver March 26.

Hopefully the weather will cooperate. Getting to the show was no problem for me. My hotel was right across the street, but I guess other people live farther away. To pass the time during the storm, Karen and I have been gambling, playing cards, and pool hustling—all at once. It's been causing great confusion and consequently we're making a killing.

Actually, I heard that a few expeditions did try to make the trek to the Denver show, but most had to turn back. A five-person team from Argentina had trained for six grueling months for the event. They say their spirits were not broken and they vow to make it to the rescheduled March 26 show.

So here we are driving along, Karen, my assistant, my tour manager, and Lewis, my choreographer. We've got to make it to Seattle! Of course since we're all from L.A., where a cold snap means high 60s, none of us has warm enough clothes on.

I'm kicking myself for wearing my favorite travel sarong,

and I know Karen is questioning her tube top choice.

I'm getting a little concerned. I see cars on the side of the road abandoned by their owners. If we break down, I have a backup plan to go by sled. I've been systematically collecting animals along the way to assemble a "team." So far we've picked up one squirrel, two dogs, and something that could be a hedgehog or a possum. I'm not sure. But if he can pull, he's in. If the sled idea doesn't pan out, I don't know what we're going to do. I don't know how to build an igloo or prepare whale blubber.

Later that night, at the Paramount Theatre in Seattle

We made it in the nick of time. After using several modes of transportation, including a car, plane, and finally a collapsible canoe (that wisely I had packed just in case), we arrived safely in Seattle. It was all so worth it. The Seattle show went so incredibly well that I've become giddy. I love the people of Seattle, every single one of them. But I especially adore the people that came to my show tonight. Being onstage and making people laugh is really an amazing feeling. I wish I could explain it. I wish I could book all my fans into select venues across the country so they'd know what it's like.

I've just been informed that we're heading out to the Great White North after spending about four hours in Seattle. The only sightseeing I got to do was reading a brochure for a Space Needle tour. It sure looks neat.

March 21—Orpheum Theatre, Vancouver, B.C.

I was very excited to perform in Canada again. It's like a whole different country! Learning about new cultures is so interesting. It's very important when visiting other countries to at least try to speak their language. During my set I made sure to pronounce "about" as "aboot." It's the key to winning over Canadian audiences.

Went to dinner after the show and sampled one of Canada's local specialties: Funions. At least that's what they told us.

March 22—*Schnitzer Concert Hall, Portland, Ore.*

Well, I'm back in the United States of America, in a beautiful city called Portland. It's taken a bit of getting used to, after my whirlwind international experience.

I've been on the road for almost two weeks now. I miss my animals. I wanted to bring them along, but then my "posse" would include mostly cats and dogs. I think a posse is considered cooler if it's primarily people. Gotta wrap this up; we head out to San Francisco in the morning and I'm going to need about twelve hours of sleep so I can make it up those hills.

In case the crowd demanded a tune, I brought my auto-harp onstage with me.

March 24—*Davies Symphony Hall, San Francisco, Calif.*

I always love visiting San Francisco. I lived here so long ago, when I was just a penniless stand-up comic just starting my career.

I took a cable car to see where I used to live. It's amazing, as you get older, how much smaller everything seems. Turns out, my old apartment was actually a galvanized steel garden shed (8'W x 3'D x 5 1/2'H) from Sears. I've come such a long way. For lunch I ate all the famous local foods, all at once. Rice-a-Roni (the San Francisco treat), Ghirardelli chocolate, sourdough bread, and a refreshing glass of wheatgrass juice.

Afterward, I felt a little queasy, so I clipped on my safety rope and made the steep ascent back to my hotel.

Davies Symphony Hall is a perfect place for comedy, because symphonies are always so damn funny. I came prepared.

March 30—Majestic Theatre, Dallas, Tex.

It's my last night in the Lone Star State. You know, what they say about Texas is true. Everything is bigger. The food portions, the hats, the bed-linen thread counts. Remember that TV show *Walker, Texas Ranger*? That was HUGE. I rest my case.

O.K., here's more proof that everything's bigger in Texas. You know those teeny tiny miniature shampoo bottles you get in hotels? In Texas they come in five-gallon jugs which makes stealing them a logistical nightmare.

April 2—Dodge Theatre, Phoenix, Ariz.

Each night, at the end of the show, I've been doing a little Q & A session with the audience. It's fun, and since I've been talking nonstop, it's nice to give somebody else a chance. The people's questions range from wanting to know the status of my latest projects to their asking me to define the molecular structure of certain kinds of cheese. Not all the questions are ones I can answer. But I always try.

April 4-6—Wiltern Theatre, Los Angeles

The Wiltern Theatre is incredibly beautiful. It was originally called the Historic Wiltern Theatre when it was built in 1931. Now it's just called the Wiltern Theatre, without the "Historic."

Why would they have called a building that was just built "historic," anyway? Would you call a brand-new restaurant

Ye Olde T.G.I. Friday's? I think not.

April 10—Palace Theatre, Columbus, Ohio

Had a splendid show at the Palace Theatre and then back to my hotel room to get some rest. I am getting so used to living in hotels now. They're like a second home to me. I'm trying to organize a block party on my floor, but so far no one has responded to my flyer...

April 20—Symphony Hall, Atlanta, Ga.

It's so nice to be back in the South, back on familiar turf. Atlanta is one of the friendliest towns around. Everything is "yes ma'am" and "no ma'am. My favorite is yaw'l (which I still use). It's such an economical way to talk. "Y'all goin'?" is so much easier to say than, "Are you presently considering departing?"

Went to a Krispy Kreme donuts. The woman behind the counter was amazingly pleasant. In L.A. if you go into a store it's never like that. At the end of a purchase you say, "Thank you for letting me shop in your store." To which the shop person usually replies, with a shrug, "Whatever."

April 15—Tower Theatre, Philadelphia, Pa.

Do you know how long it's been since I've had a home-cooked meal? When you're on the road you eat every meal out. Every one. All I want to do is make myself a tuna melt and eat it standing up in my kitchen. I almost never order room service when I'm touring because it's hard to justify eating a $10 boiled egg.

April 26—Massey Hall Toronto, Ont.

Well, back on the plane again. Being in a different city every night is getting kinda wearing. So much packing and unpacking. By the time I've put everything away it's time to pack it back up and go.

I do make sure to keep each room I stay in neat and tidy. The whole "trashing" thing isn't really my style. Instead I like to leave a little something behind to make the room just a bit nicer. Sometimes I leave a houseplant. Or, as I did in my hotel in Toronto, I repainted the bathroom. I chose a charming French Blue, which I then "ragged" over with a vibrant Sunburst Yellow. I sure hope the hotel management appreciates it.

April 27—Benedum Center, Pittsburgh, Pa.

I've been on the road now for almost two full months and today I finally got around to writing some postcards. Now if I just had time to get stamps…maybe I'll get them when I'm back in Los Angeles.

I wanted to see the Andy Warhol Museum (he was born in Pittsburgh) but didn't have time, so I just popped into a local supermarket and contemplated the Campbell's Soup section. It was the best I could do.

April 28—State Theatre, New Brunswick, NJ

The show was sold out—what a great night! Next stop is New York City to tape my HBO special at the Beacon Theatre.

The next time I write I'll be in NYC, "the city that never sleeps." I'm a tiny bit concerned because I don't want my audience to be sleepy. I need them to be alert and on top of their game. I hope New York takes a nap before my show.

May 1-2—Beacon Theatre, New York, N.Y.

Just finished taping the show for HBO at the Beacon

Theatre. Before the show I had a meeting with the director from HBO. The man has incredible insight into his craft. When I asked him, "What's my motivation?" he thought for a moment and then responded simply, but with great conviction, "Be funny." Let me tell you, those are two powerfully inspiring words. Well, actually his complete answer was, "Look, I don't have time for this. It's a stand-up show, right? Just be funny, for God's sake." But I knew what he meant.

May 5, 2003

I'm finally home! The tour is over and the HBO show is "in the can." It's hard to adjust to being in my own house after living in hotel rooms for so long.... When I dial "zero" on my phone to tell the front desk that I need more towels they hang up on me. It's weird. Anyway, I don't think I'm going to tour again for a long, long time. Not unless I can beam myself to the various destinations. When some sort of transporter device has been invented, tested, and sold to the public, I'll go on tour again.

I'm thinking maybe early spring 2086.

Ellen Degeneres is a writer, actress, comedian, and the Emmy Award-winning talk show host of her nationally syndicated talk show The Ellen Degeneres Show. *She has won several awards for her accomplishments on stage, film, and in the literary world including a Peabody Award, multiple People's Choice Awards, and a Kid's Choice award for her portrayal of Dory in the Academy Award-winning animated film* Finding Nemo. *Ellen's first book,* My Point...And I Do Have One, *instantly made* the New York Times *bestseller list, as did her second,* The Funny Thing Is, *from which this was excerpted.*

* * *

The Robbery-Free Plan

He was too clever for their own good.

FOR YEARS MY HUSBAND AND I HAD A PLAN FOR NOT getting robbed when we traveled together. It was a simple plan: he carried all of our money.

Our reasoning? At six feet, two inches and 220 pounds, West is a big guy. With large arms and a balding head, he can look imposing. In the developing countries we visit, he often towers above the locals. Certainly, we thought, a thief would think twice before picking his pockets. For years the plan worked beautifully.

There was, however, one critical flaw in our thinking. And after nine robbery-free years of travel, we found ourselves in a foreign country with absolutely no money.

We were celebrating our wedding anniversary with a trip through southern Africa. We dived with great white sharks on the rocky, cold coast of Gansbaai, South Africa. Then we flew to a dusty game reserve on the border of Kruger National Park where we saw the Big Five, a moniker given to the five most dangerous animals to hunt on foot. Lions, elephants, leopards, rhinos, and massive Cape buffalo with their upturned horns stood feet from us as we sat in awe in the back of an open Land Rover.

No one we'd met in our travels had been friendlier than the people we met in South Africa. Coetzer, our game ranger, expertly tracked Africa's incredible wildlife and looked as if he were having convulsions as he laughed at my and West's playful banter. When we arrived in Johannesburg, even the man who helped us with our bags at the airport waited with us to make sure that West and I caught the right bus. Nothing in the country resembled the warnings I'd read at home about crime in Southern Africa's most developed nation.

After an overnight stay in Jo'burg, as locals affectionately call it, we were flying to Zambia. Before leaving, we decided to exchange some money at the airport. As we reached the exchange counter, West opened his wallet, and I saw a worried look pass over his face. "Uh, just a minute," he said to the clerk.

Still holding his wallet in his hand, he stepped away from the counter. I followed him. "Why don't you sit down," he said, gesturing toward a row of chairs just inside the terminal.

In the fourteen years I'd known him, West had never asked me to sit down to receive news. My mind began to reel. I thought about the last time we'd used cash. It was that morning at the airport. Had the man who helped us with our bags grabbed money out of West's wallet? Had someone at the restaurant last night?

I couldn't take the silence. "What is it," I asked.

"I left some money in the hotel room," he whispered.

"Oh," I said relieved. "How much?"

"All of it."

"What!"

"I didn't want to carry it all to dinner last night, so before we left, I hid it under the lamp on the desk."

"Under the lamp?"

"I didn't think anyone would look there. I forgot about it this morning."

We had checked out of our hotel room more than two hours ago and taken a taxi to the Johannesburg International Airport, one of the largest airports in Africa.

West and I had weaved our way past the maze of shops and restaurants, checking in for an international flight and clearing security. A surly immigration officer had stamped the pale green sticker in our passports showing that we were leaving the Republic of South Africa. In thirty minutes we would board a plane that in all likelihood already held our checked bags.

I thought for a moment. The hotel was close to the airport. If we could get a taxi—a very fast taxi—maybe we could get there and back with just enough time to make our flight. West agreed we would try. But first we had to find the exit.

We hurried from one end of the crowded terminal to the other, dodging other travelers and looking for a neon exit sign. Of course, the thing about airports is: once you've cleared security and immigration and checked your bags onto a flight they expect you to leave on a plane. There was no exit.

I rushed back to the surly immigration officer. Waiting for his line to clear, I conjured the sweetest smile I could muster. Although in my panic, I undoubtedly looked deranged.

"Excuse me. If we need to leave the airport, where would the exit be," I asked.

"What do you mean," he said.

"We've left something in our hotel room, and we have to go back and get it," West said.

"When does your flight leave?" he asked.

"In thirty minutes, but our hotel is just down the road," West said.

"Did you check any bags?" he asked.

"Yes," I said.

"You can't leave the airport."

"Please it's very, very important," I begged.

"You'll have to go to the ticket counter and get your bags off the flight," he said. "You can't leave until you do that. Do you understand me?" he lowered his head, narrowing his eyes to make his point clear.

By my estimate we had just enough time to get to the hotel and back. We didn't have time to wait in line at the ticket counter and explain to the agent why we had to leave. I looked directly into his eyes. The rest of the country was lovely. How bad could the inside of a South African prison be anyway?

"We will. Absolutely," I lied.

"All right," he groaned. "There's an elevator past the exchange office on your left. Take it down one floor. Then go through security."

When we exited on the floor below, the X-ray machines were straight ahead. And behind them was a long line of travel-weary passengers staring straight at us. The only way out, it seemed, was to go backwards through security. I thought about the times I'd scoffed at travelers trying to cut in line to avoid missing a flight. How ridiculous, I'd thought. I probably even gave them a look of disbelief. Now, I scanned the faces ahead of us for signs of sympathy and found none.

We rushed up to a guard who stood watching travelers collect their belongings off the belt. "We need to get out," West said.

He looked at us incredulously.

"Please," I begged.

A guard on the other side stopped the oncoming flood of passengers, while West and I squeezed past them, trying not to notice their outraged stares. We rushed through the halls of the sprawling airport. When we reached the ticket counter, I turned to West and whispered, "Look away."

"Don't we have to get our bags?" he asked.

"Hell no, we don't have time for that."

We wound our way through the second floor, trying not to look panicked. For once I wished that West wasn't the biggest guy in the crowd. After all, a large bald man running out of an airport doesn't exactly scream "Enjoy your flight!"

After we cleared immigration again, this time on the first floor with a handful of arriving passengers, we finally reached the sliding doors that opened to the sidewalk. I ran outside and flagged down the first taxi I could find.

I'm not a city dweller so my idea of hailing a cab comes from too many Hollywood movies, where a wave and a "Taxi" is all it takes to get a ride. But as I slid into the back-seat, another man approached us. He fussed at the driver who began to argue back. From the exchange I understood we were supposed to wait at a taxi stand for the next available cab.

Normally, I'm a rule follower. If someone with the least amount of authority, the mailman for example, tells me to do something, I do it. But seeing as I'd just lied to an immigration officer, I was feeling emboldened—and more than a little frantic.

"Please," I begged. "We can't wait. We have to get to the Holiday Inn fast."

The man said something to the driver then reluctantly slammed the door. The taxi sped away from the curb, lurching into traffic. The driver weaved in and out of lanes, delighting at every chance to sling West and me from one side of the car to another. We had, after all, asked him to drive like a maniac, and he wasn't about to disappoint us.

At the hotel, West and I jumped out of the car. "We'll be right back," West said.

We burst into the lobby to the stares of the hotel staff. "Get the key and meet me upstairs," West said as he turned and raced up the lobby stairs.

When I reached the second floor, housekeeping was two doors away from our room where West waited outside. I swiped the card and threw open the door. West ran inside and lifted the lamp on the desk. There beneath it, folded into a bulging stack was more than $600 in cash. Feeling like we'd just won the lottery, I watched as West tucked all of the money into his empty wallet.

Our drive back was a repeat of the racecar rally that had gotten us to the hotel so quickly. At the airport we climbed out of the car, paid the driver and tipped him well. Admittedly, his tip didn't have as much to do with his driving skill as the fact that we were just happy to have money to pay him.

After clearing immigration for the third time that morning, we made it to the gate just as boarding began.

Although we made the flight, I wasn't quite ready to let the ordeal go. Later, all I could see in my head was the image of West putting our cash back into his empty wallet. "Honey, would you hand me some of that money?" I asked.

Kelly Watton is a freelance writer living in the Atlanta area. Her essays have appeared in books by Travelers' Tales and Lonely Planet. Her articles have appeared in newspapers across the country.

* ✱ *

Swooning for Swami

You've got to wonder about a guy's intentions
when he shows up carrying his own mattress.

I WAS IN THE COURTYARD OF A GUESTHOUSE IN
Haridwar, a holy Hindu city north of Delhi, waiting for the
yoga master who was to be my guide. I was here to cover the
yoga festival that reportedly happened every February on the
banks of the Ganges in nearby Rishikesh. The guide was to
help me navigate the crowds and arrange interviews.

Mr. Aroop was not what I expected. With his long dark
hair tied in a ponytail and a weatherbeaten leather jacket
atop a tunic and pyjami, he bore a striking resemblance to
actor Steven Seagal. Under his arm was a yoga mat that
looked as if it had been rescued from the floor of a crack
house. Still, there's something faintly suggestive about a
white cotton mattress no matter how filthy it is.

We headed for the car and, unlike other guides during my
preceding ten-day stint through India, Mr. Aroop headed for
the backseat instead of up front by the driver. He slid in beside me, sitting very closely.

I stared out of the car window and tried to appear ho-hum.
The streets were teeming with pilgrims. Located at the
foothills of the Himalayas, the city is a major pilgrimage site

for Hindus who travel to bathe in the sacred waters of Ganges. According to Hindu religion, spending one night in Haridwar is the equivalent of gifting 1,000 sacred cows.

Within moments, I heard chanting.

The guide's eyes were closed as though in deep contemplation. As he hummed, I took a closer look. In fact it was hard not to stare. He really was a babe. Long eyelashes and a strong jawline, he could have been a model.

Previous guides during visits to Agra, Jaipur, and Delhi had been either lacicousancient academics who declared themselves descendents of the Raj or hustlers intent upon squeezing in an endless parade of carpet shops. I couldn't help thinking how positively rosy my day was becoming.

"No harm in some eye candy," I thought with an unwarranted amount of lascivious glee.

Suddenly, there was a sudden lull in the chanting

"How do you feel?" he whispered in my ear.

"Um, good. How about you?" I mumbled embarrassed as though he'd been reading my impure thoughts.

"Very, very good," he hummed, resuming his chanting. Well, he might not be much on talking but there were obvious compensations. Soon we neared our destination, the town of Rishikesh, best known as a hub for New Age devotees. Considering a festival was supposed to be taking place, the streets were remarkably empty.

"What can I do for you?" asked the guide.

"Remember? The yoga festival?" I prompted.

"Yoga festival not until next month," he said, with finality. Great, the tourism organizers had been off by not just a few days but a whole month.

"You do yoga on river bank?" he asked. Reluctant to downward-dog it alone on a riverbank, I struggled to think of an alternative.

"Puffer shop, maybe?" he asked.

"What's that?"

"Place for smoking opium," he said, pointing out several men with serene faces sitting cross-legged at the side of the road. I'd assumed they were wise sages.

"No, those gentlemen are opium addicts," he said.

"And those?" I asked pointing to a trio of holy-looking men also seated cross-legged.

"Begging hermits."

He stood, arms behind his back, looking out across the blue waters of the Ganges, the breeze blew his *kuma* taut against his body. He was a very buff looking chap.

"Exactly what kind of yoga do you specialize in?" I asked. He was obviously no scrawny aesthetic, like the hippie teacher back home.

"Fighting yoga. I'm a big boy," he said, pointing below his waist. "My legs very strong."

"I'll say," I thought, taking a quick glance at the outline of his well-formed thighs.

"When did you decide to get into yoga?" I asked, taking out my notebook thinking I could get some kind of story out of the looming day.

"When I was young, I was very naughty and too proud," he explained. "In order to enter the path of yoga you need discipline. So I learned weaponry—daggers, sticks, fists."

Great, first he's a tough guy and now he's a bad boy, too, I thought.

"What kind of tours do you usually offer?" I asked.

"I am not guide, ma'am," he said, with an expression that blended hurt and insult. "I am astrologer, spiritual adviser, guru, and yoga master. I can penetrate you fundamentally."

"What?" I asked, not sure I'd heard correctly.

"Astrology reading," he said.

"Um, do you have many clients?" I asked.

"Very many. Why so many questions?"

"I'm a journalist. Didn't anyone tell you?" I answered. Based on his look of disgust, I assumed not. I didn't have the guts to tell him that my original plan had been to investigate Hasya Yoga—laughing yoga. It was a far cry from fighting yoga.

Finally agreeing on a morning of spiritual discourse followed by an astrological reading, we began strolling the streets. Enroute, we passed several Western women in long white robes, each accompanied by a personal guru. Their glances at their consorts were far from chaste.

I began to wonder about the pairings. Was it possible that there was more than spiritual discourse going on? After all it had been a sex scandal that caused the Beatles to turn their backs on Maharishi Mahesh. Was it possible I had inadvertently hooked up with a rent-a-gent?

Before I could finish my thoughts, I realized rapport with the guru was fast deteriorating. He was obviously finding my note-taking annoying. A low point occurred at Swarg Ashram, where I asked him to repeat the spelling of the "Umakurina" temple.

"You make urine here," he repeated slowly, watching my pen move across the notepad.

He was giving me directions to the ladies toilet.

The atmosphere between us deteriorated quickly after that. It became increasingly quiet.

"Perhaps some lunch?" I suggested brightly.

We headed to a nearby restaurant. He said something to the proprietors and they looked at me as though expecting me to ask them to be organ donors. I quickly perused the menu.

"And you?" I asked encouragingly.

"Nothing," he said staring fixedly at a statue of Krishna as though willing divine intervention to transport him away.

"Just tea for me," I said. The charm of his flashing eyes had worn off. The guru thing was evidently not for me. Only two hours had passed yet I just wanted to head to my room and read a paperback.

But it was time for my penetration—my astrological reading. Swami and I took a seat on the terrace overlooking the Ganges. He immediately launched into the reading.

"Have you had your vehicle accident yet?"

"Er, no," I said.

"Too bad," he said, shaking his head sympathetically. "You will suffer much pain. After five years you will wish for death."

A few more inauspicious prophecies later, we headed our respective ways. I'm not sure which of us was more grateful.

The next day though, I spotted the swami again. He was wearing a black turtleneck sweater and performing a handstand yoga asana on the hotel's terrace. I couldn't help stopping to take a look. As a breeze wrapped the pyjami around the contours of the swami's body, despite the differences of the previous day, I had to admit one truth.

His butt was impressive even upside down.

Michele Peterson lives in Toronto where she often contemplates taking up the study of yoga. She is a contributor to major publications such as MoneySense, Toronto Star, Globe and Mail, Boston Herald *and* The Christian Science Monitor.

* ✳ *

California Extract

She's about to go native.

AFTER YEARS OF SEARCHING I MAY HAVE FINALLY FOUND the perfect place to live, although I haven't moved in yet so I can't be entirely sure. An hour and a half north of San Francisco, in Sonoma county, in a town with the gumption to call itself Camp Meeker, I'm going to rent a room in a house entirely surrounded by redwoods. My bed will be in a glass-encased loft so all around me will be thousand-year-old giants. Faith Fauna is the name of the woman who owns the house, although I'm sure that can't be her real name. I saw her ad yesterday on a bulletin board in Occidental:

LOOKING FOR VEGAN HOUSEMATE TO SHARE LOVELY
HOUSE IN TREES, NON-SMOKER, MUST LOVE ANIMALS,
NO PETS (SINCE I HAVE CATS), $350/MONTH.

The ad also had a map showing where the house was and a phone number for a health food store in Santa Rosa where Faith Fauna works. Faith Fauna sounded very cheerful on the phone and thought I did, too. When she asked if I was vegan, I told her honestly that I eat cheese sometimes but have been planning to cut it out anyway. Also, I occasionally have a weakness for ice cream, although it usually makes me feel terrible afterwards, so I'd definitely cut that out too. I drove a mile down the winding forested Bohemian Highway from Occidental until I came to an old wooden sign that stretched above the road saying CAMP MEEKER painted in white. I had trouble getting Marcia (my car) up the steep narrow roads into Camp Meeker, and since I was early in meeting Faith Fauna, parked, and walked around the place. Camp Meeker isn't really a camp, although it was when it was founded in the nineteenth century as a lumber camp, but it isn't really a town either. It's a cluster of about three hundred houses hidden beneath a dark forest where a few roads roller coaster through it like an accident waiting to happen. Most of the houses are small and appear even smaller since they're dwarfed by three hundred foot redwoods. Most of the houses are made of wood, don't get a lot of sunlight, and look as if gnomes live in them. I saw kids playing in a big creek which snakes through the settlement and they wanted me to join them. The place isn't big enough to have its own general store, but a post office sits beneath the trees, in a trailer. When it was time to meet Faith Fauna, I walked up about fifty steps to get to her house and once inside, knew immediately it was where I wanted to live. Luckily, she felt I belonged there, too, and said I could move in immediately.

When I wake up this morning, I pack my things, and take off in Marcia for my new home. I love the drive from Sebastopol to Camp Meeker, first passing rolling meadows of California poppies and apple orchards, then winding higher through a dark forest beside a brook, then passing through Occidental, an historic village surrounded by towering trees and full of old Italian restaurants and art galleries. When I get to Faith Fauna's, she's waiting to help me unpack, not that I have any furniture. In fact, that's our project for today, to buy a futon mattress for my room, and a used couch for her living room. In Faith's truck, we drive over hilly country roads lined with vineyards to Santa Rosa and find a used, slightly weathered couch, which Faith says she'll cover with a Guatemalan blanket; and in a futon store, I buy a bed for myself. Faith also takes me to the Santa Rosa health food store where she's a manager, and introduces me to her friends working there, all vibrant student types, full of bubbly enthusiasm, wheatgrass juice, and detailed plans to change the world.

We carry the furniture up all the steps to the house with the help of a friendly neighbor, Jack, who seems to have a crush on Faith, although with his extensive beer gut and the licorice hanging out of his mouth, he hardly seems to be her type. Jack tells me he used to be a logger further north and is now trying to make a living selling used books on the internet. "Oh, so that means you get to read a lot of books," I say. No, he tells me. He gets his mother to read them, rate them, and write a review for the internet. "That way," he says, "my mother has something to do, and I get free quality control for my product." I laugh, although I'm not sure he's kidding. In any case, Jack seems like a jovial, bighearted guy and offers to show me his book collection some day.

Inside, Faith says she's going to cook us a specialty of hers. Most vegan food is delicious and I wonder what she'll make. It turns out her specialty tonight is whole wheat pasta with beet sauce. "This will transport you to another place," she tells me. I take a bite and sure enough, it does: a Siberian labor camp. However, the vegan brownies we have for dessert are scrumptious. As we drink blueberry tea, Faith tells me about growing up in Florida, how she used to follow the Grateful Dead across the continent in a van, and how she was able to buy this house when her father left her money he'd gone to jail for in the savings and loan scandal. After dinner, we continue talking on the new couch in the living room, sharing bad date stories, and laughing about how hard it is for women in their thirties to find the perfect guy. I like Faith.

I go to bed thrilled with my new surroundings among the redwoods, and sink into my new cushy futon in the glass-enclosed loft. Rain falls gently all night, splashing through the leaves off the mighty dark branches just outside my open window. I inhale misty cool air, taking deep breaths of California, and feel a familiar, wild happiness.

After several days, I'm learning a lot about Faith Fauna. Faith Fauna is an animal rights activist, strict vegan, and an Earth First! member. She has secret meetings in her home she thinks are monitored by the FBI, and she owns six cats, most of them vicious bird killers which seems to counter her animal rights stance since every day one of the cats deposits a dead bird on the kitchen floor. Since she's a vegan, she doesn't want any animal products in her home, except dead birds I guess, so I'm not allowed to bring any ice cream into the house, or butter, or even my old suede jacket. I don't mind actually. I'm feeling very healthy.

Faith Fauna has many interesting friends: Egrett, who likes to come by on the full moon; Saffron, who looks like one of Charlie's Angels; Feral, who lives in a teepee; Cool Mama; a guy named Jenny; Sha-na-na; and Anarchy. Anarchy lives in redwood trees to keep them from being chopped down. She needs a bath. Anarchy stinks.

Last night, I burned one of Faith Fauna's cats. I've never

been a cat lover—the hair, the dander, the bird killing, the litter, the unspoken demands, the attitude. But I certainly didn't mean to harm this cat. The cat was on top of the stove when I wanted to turn on an element. Faith Fauna lets her cats go wherever they please. The cat was bugging me up there looking exactly like it didn't give a crap so I turned the gas stove to high, thinking I was turning on the front element when it actually turned out to be the back one. I only wanted to startle the cat. When the back burner flared up, a yellow flame immediately transferred to the cat and a good chunk of the cat's fur went into flames for a few seconds. The curious thing was, the cat didn't care. It just stood up, stretched, and jumped off the stove. Ten minutes later I was watching a video—*Tootsie*, which I haven't seen in years—and the cat curled up on my lap. I noticed a substantial patch of missing hair along its side.

It's two days later and Faith Fauna is taking me on one of her political protests with her political friends, a highly-impressionable-to-conspiracy-theories bunch with good hearts and disheveled bird-nesty hair. We're participating in a demonstration against biogenetic engineering by performing street theater in front of Safeway, with people dressing as giant tomatoes who run away from a mad scientist with a bovine growth hormone injection. Other people are dressed as pigs with fish fins coming out of their heads, or vegetables with animal noses. My job is to video all of this, which means I get to enjoy myself without dressing as a mutant turnip. When some of Faith's friends run into the store to attach stickers on baby food saying, GMO CONTAMINATED!, the manager chases them outside. We make the local news.

Tonight, I'm in my bedroom writing when there's a knock at the door. Faith isn't home so I get up to answer it and even before I get there, I hear, "Anyone home? Anyone home?" coming from a high-pitched voice fraught with tension. When I open the door, a woman, looking to be in her mid-forties with long black and white frizzy hair floating down her back like a wild mane, is stroking a cat, perhaps one of Faith Fauna's cats—I haven't got these cats sorted out yet. I invite her in and she asks what kind of tea we have. We go into the kitchen. "Well, let's see. There seems to be all the regular herbal ones, and Chinese sorts of things. How about jasmine?" I say, thinking it might calm her nerves. Or maybe that's chamomile.

"I want to try to get pregnant, but not until January," she says out of the blue.

I look at her, this woman whose adolescence seems to have congealed beneath the wrinkles of middle age, then I look down at the boxes of teas in my hand. "Then do you need a special tea for that? For fertility or something?"

"Yeah, probably, but I told you I don't want to get pregnant until January. If I wait till January to get pregnant, then I'll give birth to a Virgo Rabbit. I want a Rabbit to get along with a Pig. I'm a Pig and so is my son. Chinese astrology."

"Oh, right."

"I definitely don't want to give birth to a Rooster. I hate Roosters. My ex-husband's a Rooster. Roosters are assholes."

"Oh, so who do you want to have the baby with?"

"My ex-husband."

"The Rooster?"

"Yeah," she says, as if it's obvious.

I stare at her hair, how it looks like an unruly multidirectional headdress. "Well, why are you telling me this?"

"I tell everybody this." She speaks in a tone which tells of ongoing bitterness, a tone which discourages further

questions. I boil water for the tea. Luckily, just then, Faith returns home with a guy named Earle who works with her at
the health food store. Earle is a poet, and I suspect that's not
his real name since he's only 24. While we're drinking green
tea and eating hemp carob muffins, Earle, the Chinese astrology woman, and Faith get into a conversation about how
the FBI introduced crack cocaine and guns into the ghettos
of New York City to get rid of all the non-whites. It seems
a little far-fetched to me, but under the circumstances, all I
can do is go with the flow.

I've now escaped back into my room. O.K., so it's a little
flaky here, but it can be flaky anywhere. Just two years ago
in Guelph, Ontario, I lived with three friends in an old
Victorian house where the vegetarian landlady downstairs
came upstairs once a week, ostensibly to vacuum, but really,
to sift through our trash for evidence we'd eaten meat—
frozen chicken wrappers, old torn-up recipes. She wanted a
vegetarian household since she claimed dead animal flesh
upset the energy balance of the house, disturbed her dreams,
and stunk up the kitchen. We never did eat meat while living there but she didn't believe us, insisting she kept feeling
a suspicious vibe of carnage coming down through the ceiling. Her husband, an anemic-looking waif of a man who
hardly spoke, placed copies of the appallingly-written
Celestine Prophecy on each of our beds when we moved in,
explaining it was required reading for anyone living there.
Our beds, incidentally, all had to be facing north, something
to do with the magnetic pull of the earth. The landlady
eventually evicted us because she "couldn't handle" the negative energy seeping down into her "living space," negative
energy aimed at her. Come to think of it, she was probably
right about that part.

No, California doesn't hold a monopoly on flakiness. And

besides, not everyone in this state is like these people I've met at Camp Meeker. It's just one Californian world within many. I just have to meet more people.

I'm now meeting more people, at a dinner party in Sebastopol at the home of a botanist named Gerry Green. (Does everyone invent a name for himself around here?) When each guest arrives, Gerry Green tapes the Latin name and common name of a plant on our foreheads and we try to guess which plant we are by going around to each other saying things like, "Do I flower?" "Am I deciduous?" "Do I attract spruce bud worm?" I keep saying, "Can you smoke me?" which people only laugh politely at, so I start saying, "Do I smell nice?" and people sniff me. It's actually kind of fun in a nerdy kind of way. It turns out I'm a sugar maple, which I think Gerry Green chose for me on purpose, thoughtfully. I have to ask about forty-five questions before I get it, which is strange since I grew up with a giant old sugar maple right in our front yard, a maple that was like a best friend, that I did handstands against, climbed, and even, when I was eleven, gave a special name to—Lady Louise of D'Austriana—a maple that crashed down in a tornado five years ago right in front of my eyes, a loss that was like a death in the family. Maybe I fail to guess a sugar maple because there aren't any out here. I'm sure I must be a sequoia or a California sycamore or a juniper or cypress or something. When it finally hits me to say, "Do I turn red?" everyone shouts out, "Yes!" as if they can't believe it has taken me this long to guess, making me actually turn red myself. The whole experience has a strange affect on me, saddens me a little being so far away from sugar maples and knowing that if I lived here, I wouldn't see them anymore.

The people at the party are all friendly, fun and intelligent and I keep thinking that they could be my new friends. At the same time, I keep thinking that I already have friends back home and in making new ones, would I be replacing the old? I don't want to lose my old friends, but in moving here, I know that gradually over time, I'd drift away from friends I once knew. Also, how long would it take to break into this new group of friends? Could I really do that? I feel like such an outsider to them. I don't have the clues and codes for this culture. It's hard to know what questions to ask, where to even begin. On the other hand, I'm still a traveler here and being a traveler, I'm out of context so I relate to people in a way I'd never relate to people back home. These Californians are as much a curiosity to me as I am to them. Over time, we'd become real people to each other. For now, our encounters are like travel encounters, inspiring and entertaining, but limited in that we only see the glossy outside.

As I'm thinking about all this, a woman named Cheron sits next to me and tells me she's also just moved here, from upstate New York. She's an artist who turns cutlery into sculptures and wants to open her own studio. She's also very hygienic. She tells me that if a tall man ever comes to visit me, I should ask him to sit down on the toilet to urinate rather than stand, because tall men always splash and get their pee all over the bathroom which is dangerously unsanitary. She's even seen this on Oprah.

I'm not sure I could be friends with Cheron.

Even though some of the people I've met can be a little extreme, I do like it here. I've always dreamed of living by the ocean and here I am—it's just over a mountain, twenty minutes away. I've always wanted to be in a place where nature is enormous, magnificent, lushly green, and doesn't include winter. I've always wanted to live in a remote wilderness but be close enough to buy Ben and Jerry's chocolate-peanut butter ice cream down the road. I've found all this here. This really is the perfect place.

If only I could wake up in the morning and tumble into the easy current of California. If only I didn't have to sneak out to my car to eat ice cream. Not that I've actually done that yet, but still...

Lauded by Time *magazine as "one of the new generation of intrepid young female travel writers," Laurie Gough is the author of* Kiss the Sunset Pig *and* Kite Strings of the Southern Cross: A Woman's Travel Odyssey, *shortlisted for the Thomas Cook Travel Book Award, and silver medal winner of* ForeWord *magazine's Travel Book of the Year in the U.S. Seventeen of her stories have been anthologized in various literary travel books, including Salon.com's* Wanderlust: Real-Life Tales of Adventure and Romance; Hyenas Laughed at Me and Now I Know Why: The Best of Travel Humor and Misadventure; *and* A Woman's World. *She has written for Salon.com,* The L.A. Times, *The Globe and Mail, The National Post, Outpost, Canadian Geographic, The Daily Express, *and* In London, *among others. She lives in Canada. (See: www.lauriegough.com)*

*

My sister Suzi and I were touring Great Britian in 1982. While riding in a luxurious tour bus through Sherwood Forest our bus had a flat tire. In those pre-cell phone years we had a long wait ahead of us. Help was on the way, just not yet. We waited and waited...after an hour or so I had to poop! There was no toilet on the bus, what to do? Suzi and I gathered our tissue supply and begged to get off the bus. The Sherwood Forest of Robin Hood's days is nothing like the Sherwood Forest of 1982. We were on a wide zooming highway...waay above a steep embankment.

We slithered and slid down the grassy hillside to the grove of trees below. While Suzi stood guard, I used my best "poop in the woods" manners, dropped trou, and did the deed. Whew! Now to negotiate the steep hill back to the bus. We had to zig and zag and crawl hand over hand. Two hours later the flat was replaced and we were on our way and we vowed to never take a bus without facilities again. We never did spot any Merry Men skulking among the trees in tights that day but at least we had found ourselves a little John!

—Shelley Hughes, "Sherwood Forest"

APRIL ORCUTT

* ✳ *

The Love Hotel

*They found a roundabout way
to get some sleep.*

WOULD STANLEY HAVE FOUND LIVINGSTONE IF HE HAD
succumbed to the sweeping spell of sleep? Or Lewis and
Clark, the Columbia River? Or Indiana Jones, the Ark of the
Covenant?

Sleep is the enemy of the explorer and the traveler. Sleep
is the dark demon that devours six, eight—and in a languid
tropical climate ten or twelve—hours a day. It rips the voy-
ager from her quest—the traveler from her trip, the explorer
from the exploration.

It lurks—always at night and during the day when it
can—ready to steal those precious travel hours.

I fight it. I wish to squeeze every minute, every second
out of my travels. I want to be out walking, observing, prob-
ing twenty-four hours a day. I don't want to miss some special feature or person or event. I fight the losing war.

I fought on the way home from an exhausting trip to
Indonesia where my husband and I had filled every moment until we boarded our plane after midnight. The flight

included a fourteen-hour layover on the tropical Western Pacific island of Guam—fourteen bonus travel hours, if we could stay awake.

Arriving in Guam at four in the morning, sleepy, unrefreshed, but eager to venture forth, we were first in line when the car rental office opened. With coffee and a Corolla, we headed out to circumnavigate the island. We drove to beaches and jungles and past American military bases. "Perhaps," I thought, "we could sleep on the beach." Warning! Caffeine wearing off!

We fought, but we found no ammunition—no coffeehouses and no coffee shops. Not even a market with chocolate-covered espresso beans.

As we searched, the heavens opened. We found refuge under a picnic shelter with two workmen, who were Chamorros—the native people of Guam—who told us the monsoon would last all day. A nearby wash began to overflow its banks. We could see nothing but water and gray. We had to accept our defeat: the double blow of monsoon and sleep deprivation destroyed our plans. We were stopped in our quest to find the character of Guam. We had lost.

Disappointed, we realized we should find a hotel and get some accursed sleep.

I mourned the gems of Guam we would miss.

When the rain eased briefly, we drove to the tourist information center, a bright office near the airport filled with pretty posters of paradise—belying the island's secrets we would soon discover. We explained to the perky receptionist in her twenties that we wanted a clean place, but we weren't looking to spend a lot of money because our flight was in five hours. Her smile brightened. "Oh!" she said. "We have hotels that rent by the hour!"

Ah-ha. We were too sleepy to be choosy; and if this young woman in a chaste mid-calf-length indigo skirt and white blouse buttoned up to her neck thought "love hotels" were O.K., we were O.K. with them, too. One was only a mile or two away.

The hotel looked anything but romantic: a gray, five-story, cinderblock monolith with no sign of life. To put a positive spin on it, no weird people skulked around the barren grounds. Perhaps the storm had repelled the nooner crowd.

Inside the dingy lobby—a jungle-green grotto about ten feet square, with fluorescent lighting and a hint of mildew— the clerk sat behind a small window through which we handed our cash. The hourly rate was only good for stays of three hours or less, and we wanted four so we had to pay the full nightly rate of fifty dollars. Without looking or speaking, the clerk slid a key toward us.

Defeated and depressed we walked down the dreary hallway toward our first-floor room. We heard only our shoes hitting linoleum and the rain outside—outside where, somewhere, lay the treasures of Guam. But we were condemned to the mausoleum, locked in by increasing torrents of rain.

When we opened the door to our room, we realized the decorator who had done the lobby and hallway had been here as well. Verdant walls were pierced by windows so narrow and so near the ceiling that no one could see out—or in. A plain, squared-off dresser and nightstands assembled from cheap particle board laminated with dark, 1970s, fakewalnut veneer rested on dun carpet. Three small bulbs glowed behind yellowed shades.

Only one feature reminded us that we were staying in something other than a forgotten motel in an obscure speck of a town long-since bypassed by the interstate: the bed.

It was round.

The bed had no headboard or bedspread—just standard white sheets and a lightweight yellow blanket across the top. No lacy, heart-shaped pillows. No mirrored ceilings. None of the bachelor pad panache of James Bond. None of the charm of a Doris Day-Rock Hudson *Pillow Talk* movie.

We chuckled and joked about deciding who would sleep on which "side."

My husband noticed TV control knobs next to the bed. He pushed the "on" button, but the television did nothing.

The center of the bed, however, started rising and falling six inches.

THUMP-A! THUMP-A! The bed bounced once each second.

THUMP-A! THUMP-A! The noise bellowed throughout the room.

THUMP-A! THUMP-A! With each rhythmic pulse, the corners of the blanket and sheet floated like the wings of a large, yellow manta ray.

THUMP-A! THUMP-A! This thunderous beast had awakened in its cinderblock cave—a gigantic libidinal organ throbbing to a beat.

If this contraption were a massage bed, it was designed by a deeply warped chiropractor in need of business. No, we concluded: it had a different purpose, one more in keeping with the carnal theme of the hotel.

The bed did serve one purpose for us: it woke us up. You can't laugh that hard and be sleepy.

Charmed with the silliest find on Guam, we spent most of our time giggling. You can always sleep at home.

April Orcutt is a California writer who's been a producer of public affairs, documentary and science television programs and a college professor who taught broadcasting and created a multimedia/web design program. She's a contributor to two books about freedom of the press in Eastern Europe and to A Woman's Asia *and* Travelers' Tales Prague and the Czech Republic. *April has slept on a dirt floor in Tibet, in a boat in Kashmir, on a bunk in the Alps, in a sleeping bag in New Zealand, on a straw mat in Bali, on a cot in Zanzibar, and on sand in Hawaii. But her favorite spot is in front of the fireplace with her husband, Michael, and their three cats. This story originally appeared in the* Los Angeles Times.

⁂

Having been unsuccessful in arranging flights out of Manila for that day, we were faced with waiting it out overnight in the city. Exhausted, we set off from the airport in search of a budget hotel. Our party was a motley crew made up of myself, my husband, my mother in-law—all awaiting flights home—and my brother in-law, his Filipina wife, and several of her relatives, who were along to see us off. Since we were all a little low on funds, someone in the group suggested that we opt for a rent-it-as-you-need-it, hooker hotel.

As we pulled into the dark, recessed parking lot of the "Cupid No-tel," a gentleman emerged from the seedy looking office and approached our vehicle. As we tumbled one by one from the over-stuffed mini-van, the man's expression changed from welcoming to perplexed. Accustomed to greeting mostly couples, he was at a loss for how to accommodate an entire family. He did his best to utter, "May I help you?" but it came out more like "You need help!" What kind of kinky freaks did he take us for?

We explained to him that our needs were innocent, and eventually the keys to three rooms were passed out. My husband and I quickly picked a key and retired to our quarters. Our room was a bright yellow number with French blue trim, but what really caught my eye was the unusual bathroom. Clearly visible from the scantily linen-ed bed was a giant, round window looking directly into the shower stall. The glassy peephole was positioned in such a way that the bather's head and feet would be cut off from view while leaving all the naughty bits in perfect frame.

As I stepped from the shower the next morning I noticed my no-longer-sleeping husband sitting up in bed, a wide grin plastered across his face. Having no idea how the other two rooms had been divided, I could only guess at how the rest of our party might be faring. Kinky freaks!

—Julia Weiler, "A Philippine Farewell"

AYUN HALLIDAY

⋆ ✳ ⋆

The Indo-Australian
Master-Pizza

When in doubt, eat local.

IF I WERE TO CITE JUST ONE LESSON GLEANED FROM
years of bumming around Southeast Asia, it'd be a toss-up
between "Beware the Australian Pizza" and "If the Monkey
Take Your Camera, Let the Monkey Have Your Camera."
Fortunately, I never met a monkey exhibiting anything more
than blasé lack of interest in my beat-up, secondhand Nikon.
Still, it seemed like good advice to have on a sign in Ubud's
Monkey Forest, as well as a maxim worthy of inclusion in
one's governing principles. Not a day goes by that I don't try
to let the monkey have my camera, at least metaphorically.

The Australian Pizza is an entirely different matter, possibly because I had a direct run-in with it. Isaac and I were
seasoned travelers by the time I ordered it in an otherwise
deserted open-air restaurant overlooking an Indonesian
surfers' beach that heavy fog had wiped clean of surfers. "Are
you sure you don't want *gado-gado* or *nasi goreng* or something?" Isaac asked when told of my choice, a good twenty
minutes or so before the establishment's scion shuffled over,
order pad in hand.

179

"I am sick unto death of *gado-gado,*" I replied peevishly. Leaving our friends had put an unexpected strain on this relationship. We'd been a cute enough couple on American soil, but were failing miserably at the trip-long assignment of being everything else to each other, too. Given that it had been more than a decade since my menu choices had been subject to parental approval, his attempt to dissuade me from the only thing that sounded good did not sit well. "And don't tell me to get *nasi goring.* I hate *nasi goreng!*"

"What about *nasi campur?*" he suggested, scanning the menu, a handwritten, poorly laminated single-sheeter.

"I don't want *nasi* anything!" I snapped. "What I want is a vacation from Indonesian food!"

"Yeah, but *Australian* pizza?" he countered, looking down the long nose I had, in less stressful times, considered pretty as a pony's.

"Jesus, they just call it that because Australia's like, what, 400 miles away or something? If we were in Mexico, it'd probably be called 'American pizza.' Look at the ingredients! 'Tomatoe saus and cheez.'"

"I just think it's smarter to stick with what the locals eat, since that's what they know how to cook."

"Yes, I know, we read the same section in the guidebook. I have been eating what the locals eat for the last five months. In fact, I seem to recall sticking with fish-ball soup when someone else was going to throw a tantrum if he didn't get to go to that Burger King in Jakarta, so if you don't mind, I think I'll go ahead and order what I want to order, just this once."

"Okaaay," he exhaled, his tone conveying that I was a) making a big mistake and b) a total bitch. Turns out he was right on both counts, though sluggish service delayed confirmation for at least an hour and a half. Mad as I was, I struggled mightily to fill that interval with conversation, terrified that we could be seen as one of those sad-sack couples with nothing to say to each other in restaurants. Not that there was anyone to see us but the waiter, who'd been AWOL so long, I worried that he had gone home.

"Maybe he's killing the chicken for your satay," I whispered with forced jollity. Isaac shrugged and gazed out at the fog. Hardly a side-splitter to begin with, the threadbare joke lacked whatever comic incongruity it might have had in our country of origin. There, the journey to the table commenced in a walk-in freezer. Here, any animal smaller than a fire hydrant was probably hanging around the kitchen in a basket, waiting for its death sentence to be carried out on the premises.

"No, I'll bet he's out picking peanuts for your peanut sauce," I revised, though Isaac's posture made clear that he was no longer even pretending to listen to my prattle. Or maybe he was, but was pretending not to, to demonstrate his loathing for me. We seemed to have hit a new low, but things were bound to improve as soon as my pizza arrived. How could they not? Nothing like a little comfort food from home to remedy a relationship sorely taxed by so much time spent joined at the hip, fighting about maps, money, and now, apparently, what I should or shouldn't order in restaurants. It was insane. The pizza would make it all better, though. Pizza was an integral part of our romantic history. We had fallen in love working in a restaurant that served wonderfully unfussy thin-crusts molten with mozzarella and other goodies. Ooh, what I wouldn't have given for one of Dave's spinach-and-garlics right then, maybe half sausage, the way Isaac liked.

"Isaac, you can share my pizza," I offered in lieu of an apology. "If it ever gets here."

No sunset was visible through that dense fog, but I imagine the sun must have been slinking toward the horizon by the time the waiter finally reemerged. In one hand, he carried a platter of satay. In the other, a pancake thickly spread with ketchup, half a raw onion bulging dead center, like a yolk.

G'day, mate! Thit's how we like 'em Down Under!

While I stared down in disbelief, Isaac silently extended a stick of satay, as if proffering his condolences. I was so traumatized that I didn't pick another fight for at least four hours.

Ayun Halliday is the Chief Primatologist & sole staff member of the quarterly zine, The East Village Inky. *She is* Bust *magazine's "Mother Superior columnist" and the author of four self-mocking memoirs*: Job Hopper, No Touch Monkey! And Other Travel Lessons Learned Too Late, The Big Rumpus, *and most recently,* Dirty Sugar Cookies: Culinary Observations, Questionable Taste *from which this story was excerpted. Dare to be heinie and head to www.AyunHalliday.com.*

C. LILL AHRENS

* ✳ *

Safariland Adventure

Not all theme parks are created equally.

THE AMUSEMENT PARK IN SEOUL, SOUTH KOREA, seemed eerily familiar—at first. After spinning in the "Teacups," our group boated through "Small World," where the animatronic dolls representing the USA wore football uniforms and skimpy cheerleader outfits. Then we gathered by the side of a wide asphalt path, across from a high wooden fence. Painted in large letters on the fence was the ride's name, "Safariland Adventure." We were first in line, waiting for a safari vehicle to arrive. Hildie's nanny appeared before me, holding my three-year-old, Spencer, for me to take. I thanked her and folded him in my arms, suddenly glad to have him back. He smelled like moist towelettes.

"Der nannies don't like dis ride," explained Hildie, her little boy in hand. "But der children tink it's der bees knees."

Grinding gears, a city bus came around the corner, painted plain white. It didn't look like a safari ride. Perhaps the white paint was a blank canvas for a future safari design.

The bus grumbled to a stop in front of us. It must have just been washed, for water trickled down the sides.

Hanging down outside each closed window was a small white paper bag. I'd seen several Korean buses decorated with ruffled white curtains or white ball fringe, but this was the first I'd seen adorned with little white bags.

"Y'all go on first," said Wanda.

"Und sit on der left," said Hildie, "Der best view."

"Thank you!"

Spencer pulled me into the first seat behind the driver. Wanda took the seat behind me, Hildie behind her. Soon the bus was filled. It started off and turned the corner. We were headed toward massive wooden gates worthy of King Kong. They swept open before us, revealing a spacious park that was a pretty good imitation of the African veldt.

"Remember the robot hippo at Disneyland, Spencer? I wonder what animals—"

"Hey!" he pointed eagerly through the windshield, "Look!"

"Ooh *wow*, sweetie!" Up ahead, on a raised wooden platform next to the road, lazed a pride of real live lionesses. They lounged like bathing beauties on a sun deck. Some lay on their backs, thighs spread wide, their soft furry tummies turned up to the sun. They groomed each other with affectionate, lingering tongues. They nibbled ears and playfully batted each other with paws the size of catchers' mitts.

"Aren't they beautiful, Spencer? Like big pussy cats." I thought of our cat Bob with a pang.

The bus slowed. The lions' ears twitched at the sound of grinding gears. Stretching languorously, they pushed themselves up to their haunches, yawned, and watched us approach.

The driver pulled up even with the platform, about five feet away, and turned off the engine. Spencer pressed his nose to the window. I skooched up close behind him. We were eye to eye with the lions. Nothing between us but a pane of glass and a small white paper bag.

"Isn't it wonderful, sweetie? They have so much room to roam, yet they choose to hang out here where we can see them up close." This was nearly a dream come true. When I was a kid I read *Born Free*, about the tame lioness Elsa in Africa, who was as free as a house cat to come and go as she pleased. I had longed for a lioness of my own. This was probably as close to lions as I'd ever get—so much better than any other "wild animal safari" I'd ever been to. Except for their teddy bear ears they looked so much like my cat Bob—golden eyes, flat dry noses, pink bristly tongues, magnificent fangs, for some reason called canines. I wondered if their fur was as soft as Bob's. I wished I could pet them. I wished I could hear them purr.

Then I heard purring. *Loud* purring. Or was it a growl?

With a deafening roar the entire pride pounced on the bus, jerking it sideways. Everyone shrieked in surprise and delight—except Spencer, his face still pressed to the glass. I

> We spent three days convincing our four-year-old that he would not be attacked by a shark in the ocean. Instead, a clam somehow attached itself to his tiny manhood. You cannot prepare for something like that. We are still in therapy.
>
> ◆
>
> —Jennifer Graham,
> "I Need a Vacation"

tried to pull Spencer onto my lap but he had a death grip on the window ledge. Lions leapt from the ground at the windows.

I laughed over the screams, "Don't be scared sweetie! They can't get us!"

Lions slashed at the bags on Wanda's and Hildie's windows. They crushed the bags against the windows with slavering jaws, smearing the glass with drool, grease, and blood. The bags were full of *raw meat*?

We kept screaming in fun—except for Spencer, who had made no sound at all. I couldn't see his expression with his face glued to the window. "It's O.K. sweetie!" I laughed, "We're safe. It's like watching a scary movie!"

KRUNK!

"Eek!" I ducked and looked up. The ceiling had dented in. Lion on the roof? Cool!

One amazing paw reached down right outside our window, swiped for the bag, missed and swiped again. From down below, another lion stretched up after our bag, snarling and snapping at the lion above us, dodging, slashing. The lower lion snatched the bag. She devoured it in the grass, paperbag and all.

The driver started the engine. The lion on the roof leapt back to the platform, tail lashing with disappointment. She'd have to wait for the next bus.

Way too soon it was over. As we pulled away, Spencer turned in my lap and stared bug-eyed at the receding lions. I hugged him, hoping he wasn't scarred for life, "Was that scary, sweetie?"

He pressed his nose to mine, looking crossed-eyed, "Yeah!" He grinned, "Let's do it again!"

I laughed. Why had I worried about him? Then I noticed my hands tingled and my heart was pounding in my ears. Despite having a great time I'd been hyperventilating. "I'd like to do it again, too," I told him, "but I don't think it's good for my nerves."

He sighed and turned back around. With my lap as an easy chair, he settled in for whatever else the future held in store. I closed my eyes and focused on deep breathing, trying to slow my heart.

Whomp! "Eep!" I yipped. Wanda had clapped me on the shoulders from behind.

"Wasn't that fun, darlin?"

"We did not want to tell you before hand!" called Hildie behind her, "It would spoil der surprise!"

Wanda shook my shoulders, her bracelets rattling my eardrums. "So? What ya think?"

"I loved it!" I said truthfully. But I was also feeling a bit faint. I breathed into my cupped hand.

"You'd never get this ride in America," Wanda drawled behind me, "Not even in *Texas.*"

Greasy, drooly, with most of the bags on the windows of the right side miraculously intact, our bus exited through a tall chain-link gate. I surmised we were headed for the bus wash. I wondered if the bus was white for the ease and economy of painting over claw marks.

BANG!

"Eek!" I ducked and looked up. The ceiling had popped back into shape. It occurred to me that everyone else had stopped screaming a while ago. I closed my eyes and focused on slow, deep breathing. After awhile, my thumping heart, tingling and dizziness began to subside.

"Hey *mom*," Spencer said, "Look!" He was pointing out the windshield.

Up ahead, on a platform on the right side of the road, lazed an ambush of tigers.

C. Lill Ahrens was a visual artist all her life until a sojourn in Korea made her a writer. Award-winning excerpts from her book-length memoir in progress, Seoul Survivor – or – Where are They Going with My Kitchen Sink? *(from which this story was excerpted) appear in literary journals and anthologies. Lill is a creative writing instructor and book doctor in Corvallis, Oregon, but her favorite teaching gig is leading writing retreats in exotic locales (so far the Oregon Coast). Lill is also a published cartoonist, an editor for* Calyx: A Journal of Art and Writing by Women, *the contest director for Oregon Writers Colony, and she belongs to three long-lived critique groups, one monthly, one weekly, and one emergency. Because Lill's brother is an airline pilot, she and her husband, Paul, have the privilege of flying standby, but are occasionally bumped for freight.*

* ✳ *

Lost in Sex Camp

When it comes to mating rituals,
one size does not fit all.

WITHIN MOMENTS OF STEPPING OFF THE PLANE AND into the Caribbean humidity, my hair expanded to the size of a circus balloon. Meanwhile, the damp air was having the opposite effect on my dress, which was now clinging to my thighs. Once aboard the bus on the way to Club Med, I scanned the surroundings, looking for my tropical paradise, but I was shocked to find there wasn't a palm tree in sight. Providenciales, known by the locals as "Provo," was a sandy, scrub-covered wasteland dotted with banks, insurance companies, and convenience stores—the kind of place that screamed, "Do your offshore money laundering here!" I was beginning to wonder if we'd landed on the wrong island until we drove through the gates of the Club Med compound. Instantly, the scenery morphed into such an explosion of palm trees and bougainvillea that I felt like I'd been escorted into a B-movie shot in Technicolor.

Filing off the bus, we were run through a gauntlet of cheering Club Med employees who did what I could only describe as the visual equivalent of squeezing the produce. The other guests seemed to enjoy the attention, but with my frizzed-out hair and stick-on dress, I couldn't run fast enough.

Our orders were to take our luggage to our rooms and report back immediately for orientation. I was directed to a complex of what looked like community-college dorms and found my room on the second floor. It had no TV or telephone, but to me all that mattered was the air conditioner in the window, which I promptly plastered myself against. Once I'd cooled down enough to peel the fabric from my thighs, I wandered over to the orientation at the open-air theater.

On the walk over, I could see the resort had been planned for optimum fun in the sun for the 600 or so guests—with its two pools, beach volleyball pits, basketball and tennis courts. Signs near the beach directed guests to the scuba shack and waterskiing dock. Practically every venue was bustling with activity, and I wondered if as much activity was going on between couples back in the rooms.

Surely the liveliest spot in the place was the orientation, a spectacle led by the village chief, a fortyish, eternally tanned Spaniard named Lulu whose long brown hair offered better coverage than her blue satin bikini. Shuffling like a prizefighter, Lulu introduced her staff—the chief of water sports, the chief of tennis, the chief of margaritas, and so on—and each was received by the audience with the kind of enthusiasm normally reserved for the Super Bowl's starting offense. She explained how to use the Club Med lingo: Staff members were GOs, short for *Gentils Organisateurs,* so named by Club Med's French management, or Gracious Organizers. Guests were GMs, or *Gentils Membres.*

Then Lulu made her announcements, punctuating them with Club Med's signature cheer—a high-pitched screeching noise that sounded like a Canada goose during mating season. Most of my travel companions already were well versed in the custom and happily screeched along with her. Try as I might, I found myself incapable of getting into the screeching spirit. In fact, the only thing the noise evoked in me was a single question: *Who are these people?*

Over the course of the week, I found out just about all I ever wanted to know about GMs. First of all, calling Club Med a "singles haven" is like calling the Sopranos a "family from New Jersey." The description simply doesn't do justice to all the complexities. Indeed, the Turkoise resort was its own erotically powered minisociety where complete strangers converged, hell-bent on finding mutual attraction. Little psychodramas played out every moment of every day—the advances and flirtations, the snap assessments (*Is he cute enough? Am I drunk enough?*), then it was either all systems go or the brush-off. Whether or not the outcome was sex (and from what I picked up in conversation, there did seem to be plenty of GMs back in their rooms getting it on), the two consenting parties tended to move on in search of more coming attractions.

But this wasn't a one-size-fits-all mating ritual. GMs naturally flocked to their own kind, which meant the resort was split squarely down the middle by age thirty, the Great Divide. On one side were the tanned and carefree twentysomethings, effortlessly working the bar, the beach, and the pool. On the other side were the over-thirties, slathered in sunblock and looking as if they were trying a little too hard to have fun.

For the younger crowd, generous amounts of frozen margaritas seemed to be the only prerequisite to a good time. The older ones, though, apparently needed actual planned activities—windsurfing classes, snorkeling excursions, water polo. Afterward, they too convened around margaritas.

And then there was me—at age thirty, sitting atop the Great Divide. Looking one direction, I knew I had left behind those days when adulthood basically meant paying your own cable bill and marriage seemed as irrelevant as a pension plan. But looking the other way, I wondered, *Was I about to become one of Them?*

For a week, at least, the answer was yes. My magazine assignment virtually assured it, since I was required by my editor to do all the activities the over-thirties were flocking to. Now, only time would tell whether I would be one of the cool people or a loser.

My baptism was immediate. The afternoon after orientation, during my first meal in the compound cafeteria, I plunged headfirst into the Club Med lifestyle. A hostess had put me at a table of over-thirties, and before I could even spear a garbanzo bean in my salad, the perky blonde to my right turned to me and said, "So, I told the tennis instructor there's, like, *no way* I'm sleeping with him. I mean, yeah, I'll fool around, but, like, if he thinks he's getting more, then, like, he's totally an idiot."

To which I could only think to reply, "I'm Suzanne. Have we met?"

The guy to my left, who looked like Barney Fife, only thinner and with a larger Adam's apple, explained that he and his roommate had developed a secret code system involving rubber bands on the doorknob, in case one of them happened to "catch some action."

Not quite sure how to respond to that conversation starter, I mumbled something about looking forward to the snorkeling and tried to remind myself why I'd wanted to go on this trip in the first place. I was, after all, in the midst of lots of guys who were highly motivated to have a fling. All I had to do was find one who highly motivated me.

Early in the week, I experienced a distinct flicker of hope. I spent an afternoon lounging by the pool in twenty-something land, where I thought I'd lucked into a handsome financial analyst with a British accent. But after a few minutes of pleasant conversation, he squeezed my biceps and said, "I never did understand why a woman would lift weights," then got up and walked away. Considering that my arms did not exactly look like Xena, Warrior Princess, I wanted to yell back, "Hey, I never did understand why a man would want love handles!" But I decided against it.

Unfortunately, that was about as good as it got. After about forty-eight hours, I'd partaken of the whole resort experience enough to conclude that the men who came to Club Med for a fling were not in the demographic of men I wanted to have flung.

Perhaps the most shining example of this was a tall, slender GM with dirty blond hair whom I encountered poolside. With no prompting, apropos of nothing, and to nobody in particular, he announced, "You know, Lance posed nude in *Hustler.*" He then dashed off to his room only to return with a copy of the magazine, which he proceeded to parade around to a group of us. I confess that, purely out of morbid curiosity, I took a glance myself. What I saw was shocking. Not the photo, but the date at the bottom of the page. This particular issue of *Hustler* was twelve years old.

I took a quick mental inventory of all the humiliating things I had done in my life and decided that none had come close to traveling with a twelve-year-old photo of myself naked.

Once I determined that all hope for sex was lost, my mood took a downturn, but I rebounded by reminding myself that, unlike the other GMs, I was getting paid to be there. For the sake of my assignment, I soldiered on with a full schedule of Club Med activities.

One morning I attended a stretching class taught by a grumpy Belgian woman who could have used a couple of assistants to help keep her breasts within the confines of her white, sequined leotard. "O.K.," she instructed, "now we bounce," which she seemed to do without moving a muscle. (Never mind that, if she had read any one of the seventy-eight versions of "Firmer Abs, Thinner Thighs" I had written, she would have known that bouncing is now considered verboten.)

Later I went to water aerobics, where the instructor directed us to form a circle and massage the person in front of us. Reluctantly, I grazed my fingers on the stooped shoulders of the Arnold Horshack look-alike ahead of me. Then I glanced back and saw that my neck was being stroked by a flabby middle-aged Frenchman whose left-side comb-over was now plastered down the right side of his face. I slithered away and sprinted to my room for a shower and a nap.

At the snorkeling venue, a GO instructed the fifty of us in line to double up, and before I could even scout out my options, a knock-kneed woman named Shirley squealed, "So, we'll be partners, right?" Our group was then herded onto a boat and transported to a coral reef about a thousand yards offshore. After we squeezed into our masks and fins and jumped overboard, I quickly discovered there were more GMs in the water than fish. Fifteen minutes later, I gave up, climbed back in the boat, and spent the next half hour relishing my time alone. I was enjoying a mininap on deck when I was startled awake by a familiar squeal. "We were supposed to stay *together*," snapped Shirley. "Those were the *rules*. That wasn't *safe*. It wasn't safe at *all*."

I couldn't believe how much I could hate someone I had known for less than two hours.

Although I fully admit the vast majority of GMs, young and old, seemed to think the resort was nirvana, I did occasionally bump into people who, like me, felt that a week at Motel 6 in Des Moines would have been preferable. One day at lunch I lent an ear to a chubby, despondent pathologist in his mid forties. He practically wept when I mentioned that my journalist status had scored me a single room. Most of the GMs had been randomly paired with roommates, and his had locked him out for three consecutive nights. "The only time he let me in," the doctor said, "was to help him find his Zoloft."

You know the movie *Groundhog Day,* where Bill Murray relives the same hellish day over and over and over again until he finally gets it right? That's exactly what Club Med eventually became to me—except I never got it right. Each day, the same activities were scheduled at the same place and the same time. At noon by the pool, the staff would line up and lead the GMs in a dance involving elaborate hand gestures and the words "sunshine," "moonlight," and "boogie." Every afternoon, the guy at the piano bar would sing the same songs in the same order. I swore that if I heard "Candle in the Wind" one more time the rest of my life, I would drown myself in a vat of frozen margaritas. The nightly entertainment was usually a musical/comedy act involving lip-synching and men in drag, with and without water balloons shoved down their tube tops.

By midweek, I'd gathered enough material for the upbeat

story I was being paid to write and began hiding in the one place on the premises that was always empty: the gym. No one had traveled to the Caribbean to use the StairMaster.

It was near the end of my trip, one night at dinner, that I was reminded of one of Grandpa Julius's favorite sayings: "Nothing's so bad that it couldn't be worse." I was seated next to Sally, a weathered blond Provo resident who was visiting Club Med for the evening out of curiosity. My jaw dropped as she told her tragic tale. Married for twenty years and living in Manhattan, she had left her husband for an artist and on a whim had moved with him to Provo, sinking all her money into a house on the island that she'd found on the internet. It wasn't until Sally and her new lover had settled in that she discovered he was a penniless alcoholic, that their tropical paradise was a scrub-covered refuge for drug smugglers, and that her dream house was worthless. Now she was stranded in Provo, unable to unload her property, desperate for customers at the beachwear shop she'd opened, and in trouble with the local government for tax evasion.

Meeting Sally gave me a new tolerance for Club Med.

If she could endure two years in Provo, surely I could handle three more days at the Turkoise compound.

But that was before I took the Sunset Singles' Cruise my editor insisted on. Last to arrive on the boat, I got stuck next to a chinless, slump-shouldered assistant tire-store manager from the Bronx whose toenails were so long they looked like guitar picks. I fled to the other side of the boat, where I ended up seated next to a woman on her fifth trip to Club Med Turkoise. She broke the ice by telling me she was "absolutely, completely sure" she had owned her two golden retrievers in a previous life.

By day five, I had discovered a coping strategy even better than the StairMaster: I was sleeping fourteen hours a day.

At dinner on the seventh and final night, I felt I had one last burst of friendliness in me, so I introduced myself to the sixtyish man sitting across the table. He had skin like beef jerky and dyed brown hair that was turning orange from the sun.

"So, where are you from?" I said, falling back on the typical Club Med opening line.

"Club Med," he said.

"No, I mean, where do you *live*?"

"Club Med."

He explained that he was "retired from pharmaceuticals" and for five years had been carting three suitcases from village to village, staying a month or two at a time, with no home base. He didn't mind that he had no access to newspapers, TV, or the outside world and did not consider his lifestyle a hindrance to building long-term relationships. Just recently at a village in Mexico, he said, he'd fallen for a Frenchwoman who had gladly quit her job in Paris to join him at Club Med. Alas, the relationship didn't work out. "After two weeks," he said wistfully, "we realized we weren't in love. Maybe it was the age difference." She was twenty-three. He sent her back to Paris and was searching for a replacement.

On the bus ride back to the airport, disappointment, particularly among the women, was palpable. Their experiences seemed to fall into two categories: Either they hadn't gotten laid, or their sex partners had discarded them like gum wrappers. That was when I realized I'd done the impossible. I'd spent the entire week at Turkoise without becoming either popular or a loser.

Suzanne Schlosberg has penned and co-penned several fitness books including Fitness for Travelers, The Ultimate Workout Log, *and* The Fat-free Truth. *Her articles have appeared in such magazines as* Real Simple, Shape, Backpacker, *and* Health *as well as the anthologies* Sand in My Bra *and* Whose Panties Are These? *Suzanne is the author of* The Curse of the Single Table, *a true story of 1001 nights without sex, from which this story was excerpted.*

, ✳ ,

Thongs for the Memories

*The phrase "Italy or bust" takes on
a whole new meaning.*

EVERYONE IS ENTITLED TO A LAPSE IN JUDGMENT. I JUST wish mine hadn't happened on the day I arrived in Italy.

A few days before my flight, I read a magazine article about these Hollywood divas who claim that wearing sexy underwear made them feel more womanly. They say this, of course, as they lounge on top of a bearskin rug, or other equally dangerous, but dead animal. How could you not feel the sensuality dripping off them? They exude sex...lewd, lascivious, seductive sex, the kind of sex men run into walls for.

I remember one particularly well-known starlet posing as the poster child for lace and satin. Her perky little breasts pushed out of their peek-a-boo bra like flesh-colored, play dough mounds. Her butt, for some reason arched unnaturally high, and she had the barest indication of a thong emerging from her well-rounded buttocks. The article was convincing, too. She swore that wearing those little angel fabrics against her skin reminded her all day long how sexy she really was.

Let's face it, my heydays are well behind me. I needed

something to bring the fire back. My husband and I were traveling to the most romantic country in the world and I thought what better place than Italia to spring this on him. I immediately went out to Victoria's Secret and spent enough money to put Victoria herself through college.

I carefully dressed that morning, slipping my breasts into a slinky black number that barely passed as a brassiere and my well-proportioned bottom into an even slinkier little black thong. I think my shoelaces had more material. On the other hand, it must have had some effect because I swear I stood taller, my breasts saluted, and my butt arched just like the movie star in the picture. The entire trip was a seven-hour romp of innuendo and cozy conversations with my husband.

We arrived in Roma and settled into a line that formed up at a counter to present our passports. I felt like the sexiest woman alive—up until I dropped my passport and stooped to pick it up. Suddenly, my privates were assaulted from the rear. Holy cow, I didn't think a cord of fabric could dive in so deep. Worse yet, my breasts dropped out of my slinky new push up bra like a load of iron ore. I was exposed at both ends.

I dove behind my husband looking vaguely suspicious to airport personnel. My rear end was being probed deeper than any gynecologist's finger while my arms wrapped conspicuously across my chest. Much as I hate them, there's a reason God created bras. Trust me, you don't want to see a forty-something-year-old woman without one. I agonized over what to do. It was a treacherous man-filled gauntlet to the nearest ladies bathroom, and there was no way to get there until I passed Customs.

Whether it was my profound embarrassment or my dubious intentions, the Customs officials kept us there a long time. Maybe it just felt that way. At that moment the only thing I was feeling was exceptionally exposed. I kept my husband in front of me as I pursed my butt cheeks ever tighter to prevent that damnable thong from violating me any further. I knew if I didn't stop the progression soon, it would have to be surgically removed.

We marched towards the bathroom at double-time, probably commanding the attention of every security camera in the vicinity. As soon as I reached the safety of a stall, buttons were unfastened, zippers unzipped, and snaps undone. I pulled a long silk scarf from my head and held it in my teeth as I tucked my breasts back into my diminishing bra then wrapped the scarf securely over the entire package.

The thong was next. With superhuman strength, I snapped the cord and pried it off my body not wanting to think of the places it had recently visited.

My humiliation finally at an end. I stepped out and heaved a deep sigh of relief.

A cleaning woman entered the bathroom at the very moment that I was leaving. She chuckled and signaled for me to wait. I paused apprehensively as she bent low and untangled the thong from the heel of my shoe.

"*Benvenuto a Italia*," she said laughing softly

Next time I travel, I'm wearing full body underwear.

Maria Zannini is a writer and graphic artist living anonymously in Texas. After this international fiasco, U.S. officials have asked her not to leave the country anytime soon. They have enough to worry about.

*

There it was, between the pages of an underwear catalog hosting thongs that promised to turn me into a winged heavenly body—a strapless, green-and-white striped sundress that hugged the model's curves and splayed out to a knee-length skirt. The keyhole opening at the top revealed just enough sexy cleavage. This dress was made for Paris and I was determined to get it there.

Soon, my friends and I were strolling amongst the sidewalk cafés of Paris, me in my perfect new outfit. A waiter's eye paid homage to the dress and an artist wished to be my boyfriend. A small congregation of old men took pause to look my way, their adoring glances affirming that the dress had found its home—*and* then it happened. An airshaft coyly awaiting my innocent tread suddenly breathed the sidewalk to life. Too late, I realized that the cool breeze beneath me had billowed my skirt into a Marilyn Monroe nightmare. My knee-length splay now hovered somewhere around my hips.

Pulling my knees together and pushing down my skirt, I bounced over to a less breezy section of the sidewalk, looking like I was in the midst of a hopscotch seizure. There was nowhere to go and nowhere to hide, so I did the only thing I could—I threw my head back and laughed. I waved to the men whose conversation had turned from normal day chatter to peep show de jour, and listened to my friends as they offered comments like "that only happens in the movies."

As we paraded back by my admirers, I kept a close eye on the sidewalk trap set before me. Success! Laughing again, the men waved to me and smiled as we passed. I waved back and considered myself lucky to have color coordinated my pistachio thong panties with the green stripes of my strapless dress. The outfit may not have clung to my curves and it may not have turned me into a winged heavenly body, but I had definitely honored the spirit of its fashion with a movie star performance.

—Tiffany Fisher, "The Paris Dress Incident"

MARCY GORDON

* ✳ *

The Sears in Uganda

She takes the wrong turn on a phrase.

PART OF THE CHARM OF LIVING IN A FOREIGN LAND IS the pleasure of breaking through the language barrier. At least for me it is. Even if I can't understand the exact words people speak, I always think I can *intuit* what they are saying. But I never expected to find myself trying to break through a language barrier in my own language, in my own country, or for it to be so stressful and taxing a situation. Who knew that moving from California to Florida could be so alien?

According to the map we were in Florida, but everyone we met stressed…"this ain't Florida…it's South Georgia, the true South." Nothing was as it first appeared or sounded. After a few weeks of people asking us if we like to drink wine I came to understand it was code of sorts to see if we were beer-swilling rednecks or refined folks who sought the finer things in life beyond a screw-top bottle. Yet aside from the code phrases, it was still a great challenge to understand much of what people were saying. I found the accents practically un-interpretable, and everyday exchanges with people suddenly became verbal labyrinths. Take for example my little chat with the cable guy:

"Yar husbin like copper tree?"

"Copper Tree? What's that, a wine?

"A watt? A whine? What you talking 'bout?"

"I thought you asked if my husband liked Copper Tree. I thought it was a wine like Copper Ridge or Turning Leaf or something like that."

"No girl, I ain't talking 'bout whine. I wants to know do he like to whack da wood."

"I beg your pardon?"

"Whack da wood!"

This seemed somewhat perverse and I was not sure where the conversation was going when I realized he was saying *carpentry*, not Copper Tree which it sure sounded like. He wanted to know if Roger liked to *work* with wood not *whack* it as I had mistakenly heard.

Next, I blundered through another dialogue with one of the electricians working on our house. He asked me if I ever went to Sears in California.

"Once in a while," I said.

"I never seen anything like the Sears out there. They so big," he said.

"Yeah, I guess they are bigger there. But the local Sears here, while not huge, certainly carries everything you might need."

"What?" he asked puzzled.

"The Sears here has a good selection."

"Sears? The stow?" (store)

"Right, weren't you asking me about the Sears in California?"

"Girl yu crazy. A'hm talking 'bout the Sears. The mountains out in California."

"The Sears Mountains?"

Then it hit me...he was saying the Sierras not the Sears! Or the See-ears as he pronounced it.

I seemed to be experiencing one gross misunderstanding after another. And I was getting a reputation with the construction crew that I was retarded. I reached the point where I was afraid to engage anyone in conversation at all. My unwitting series of gaffes and faux pas were becoming unbearable.

Then one day as I was walking down the beach with my husband Roger and our dog Bruno, something happened that helped change my attitude. As usual there was nary another person on the entire stretch of coast save for two other souls scanning the tide line for shells and shark teeth and whatnot. It was a beautiful

———) ———

One of my most memorable experiences in West Germany was a visit to the neighborhood meat market. I wanted to make a Yankee pot roast to impress my new friends.

Upon catching the butcher's eye, I pointed to a piece of meat in the cooler, and then slapping my behind, inquired "*Moooo?*"

"*Nien,*" he promptly replied. "*Oink oink.*" He smacked himself on the shoulder to indicate the cut.

Next, he reached into the cooler for a piece of meat "*Mooo,*" he informed, me while patting his chest. "*Ya?*"

At this point I purchased the meat and vowed to learn German.

◆

—AlethaLou Harmon,
"Meat Market Charades"

clear day with no clouds and a calm jade green sea warm enough to go swimming in had we been so inclined. But we were mostly there to give Bruno a little recreation.

Having a dog is an instant conversation starter and Bruno is a magnet for all sorts of people who seem to have had a chow chow in their childhood or knew someone with a chow or just know about chows from watching Martha Stewart. We passed an extremely tan woman who was collecting shark teeth and she *oohed* and *ahhed* over Bruno.

After a mile or so we turned around and came back by the same lady as before and I stopped to ask her about the shark teeth she had collected while Roger walked on with Bruno. She had just moved from Orinda in California. The exact place we had moved from!

I told her she had to meet my husband—he wouldn't believe she was from Orinda. So we walked a few yards down the beach where we found Roger engaged in a conversation with another woman who was all agog about Bruno.

It turns out that the lady talking with Roger had a chow when she was a child in a tiny little border town in Germany. But then the Nazis came along and shot all the men in the town and she and her mother fled for Amsterdam and the chow was never seen again. How she mourned the loss of that chow. "It vas the most difficult moment of mine life," she said.

No doubt, I thought.

"But now I am here in this beautiful place and the horrors of the past they are not wit me anymore. But I see dis magnificent chow and I am feeling very close to tears. May I hug him?" she asked.

Knowing that Bruno is rather skittish with strangers I was fearful that he would possibly flinch or lunge at her, but before we could say it may not be a good idea, she threw herself across him and hugged with all her might. Bruno did not budge. He let her hug him without a bit of resistance. I think it was a miracle. I thought we were all going to bust out in tears right there on the beach.

Then I introduced Laura, the woman from Orinda, to Roger. And Roger introduced the woman from Germany. Her name was Lisel. I thought that was the name of the oldest daughter in *The Sound of Music*, but I didn't want to ask.

When Laura said she was from Orinda, Lisel said, "Uganda? How fabulous. How did you come to find yourself here all the way from Uganda?"

And we all looked at each other. Laura said, "No, not Uganda, Orinda...it's in California."

"Oohh, Ya Ya, I misunderstood," Lisel said. And right then and there I wanted to hug Lisel myself, since in my mind she was a kindred spirit of the misinterpretations that had been be plaguing me on the island.

Then Lisel looked at Laura and said, "But I know you. No? I walk the beach here every day. I see you before?"

"Yes," Laura said, "I see you too."

"But I did not recognize you just now. I remember van you var white no?"

"Excuse me?"

"Now you are a regular *schwarzer* no? I think you used to be a white woman, no?"

Laura and Roger looked at me as If I could explain what Lisel was saying and oddly enough I could. I thought the term *schwarz* was a derogatory term at first, but *schwarz* means black in German and I guessed that Lisel was trying to say that Laura had become very dark, very tan.

"Oh yes," Laura said, "I have sort of overdone it in the sun."

And indeed she was very close to being a leather couch with two legs instead of four.

"Ya, ya, you are so very very *schwarz*!" Lisel said, laughing.

Then she gave Bruno another pat on the head and continued to laugh as she walked away. I watched Lisel meander down the beach and hoped that someday I would be able to embrace the world of misconceptions as charmingly as she did.

Marcy Gordon operates Bocca della Verita, a business providing marketing and editorial services to travel guide publishers. She is a contributing editor to the new Authentic Italy *series published by the Touring Club of Italy. Her writing has appeared in* 30 Days in Italy, The Thong Also Rises *and* What Color is Your Jockstrap? *She is currently working on* Come for the Wine, Stay for the Surgery, *a memoir of her adventure in the charming Italian healthcare system.*

* ✷ *

Make Mine Me

*Her cups ranneth over so she took
the girls on tour.*

MY SISTER SHOWED UP THE OTHER DAY WITH A NEW set of breasts. Bouncy breasts. Rounded breasts. Breasts that aim dead ahead with the resolve of a heat-seeking missile.

And I don't get it.

This is a woman so pathologically modest that she'd sooner be shot than be seen in her flannel, lumberjack-plaid lingerie, much less (no way!) stark naked. And yet here she is: lifting her top so all assembled—her husband, children, sisters, brothers, parents, in-laws, and dog—can witness the implant surgeon's handiwork. Braless, her breasts are mottled black and blue and brazenly shout hurt and pain. My sister beams.

"I don't mind showing everyone," she says, "because they aren't me."

Her husband Michael, feeling accused by the silence in the room, puffs for confrontation. "Trust me," he says, "I had nothing to do with it."

Acquired on the sly and to the shock of us all, Camille's new B-cup babies—$3,500 each—are the last thing on the planet she'd be expected to desire. A tomboy as a child, a teenaged athlete, a successful stockbroker, and now, a wife and mom, my sister's sleek, lean shape at its best was not the stuff of bodacious. But it wasn't uncomely either. And even through two pregnancies, countless diets, and the relentless feminine frustrations with fashion, fitness, and her "flaws," never so much as one discouraging word ever was heard from her about her breasts. There was no obvious envy of the generously endowed, no audible lament over the little loss of oomph that comes with the passing years.

Until her trip to Paris.

And now here they are: Camille's new purchased works of breastly perfection.

So, O.K., I say, recalling some stats I once read in *Time* magazine. In France, $2.9 *billion* was spent last year on lingerie, more than any other country in Europe. And a full 87 percent of French people believe these bits of silk and snips of lace are an important—yes, *important*—part of life. Is it one trip to the land of beauty and the bust and one week of a shopping spree, I ask, and you're sold on the whole French God-is-in-the-*dentelle* thing?

"Not at all," insists my sister, saying don't be ridiculous, lace isn't about God at all. "The lingerie is not *that* hot; it's just really pretty and besides, it's not about the breasts."

It's not? Well, it certainly is some bosomly vavavoom my sister now projects. And you'd think it would be eager to (forgive me) bust out around town dolled in tighter t-shirts, plungier necklines, tiny cropped tops, and bikinis of itsy-bitsy demi-cup tops—especially since Camille is so tickled by the topic of her no-sweat outpatient procedure that its grotesque and gory details—the less said, the better—is the conversation starter she won't hesitate to use. With anyone.

"It's just so interesting," she says, "because come on, it's not like they're me!"

But no. Dressed as usual in baggy blouses and camouflage sweaters and workshirts that swing unisex, Camille's new breasts could not be less interested in flaunting their fresh and oh-so-fetching femininity. Apparently, their power is more subtle; their wiles less expected. In fact, my sister's fuller, firmer new friends are about to change her life. They will take her places she hasn't been in years, introduce her to adventures she never dared try. Once the incisions heal, the tenderness lessens, and they feel more at home on her chest, Camille's new breasts will turn her into the kind of traveler I barely dare to dream of being. A woman freer. Emboldened. Gutsier, if bustier.

For instance, my sister's magical new mammaries will inspire her to climb Alaska's Mt. McKinley, at more than 20,000 feet. They will see her off to Europe for a romantic eleventh anniversary, dream of a summer sojourn to Sweden, and save for an African photo safari. Here a trip, there a trek, everywhere an airport security check...why, my sister's intrepid breasts will see to it she henceforth renounces routine and makes her life fun.

What next? I ask, eventually. Will your newly beckoning bust beg you to take-up skydiving? Urge you to join an expedition up Everest? Will it insist you leave Michael and the children to run off with a bronzed, blond hunk of barely twenty-one? "No, nothing like that," Camille laughs. "They just make me feel better about myself. Even though no one will notice and no one can tell," my sister says of the bosomly facsimiles that have that only-her-surgeon-knows-for-sure look and feel, "I did it for me. To feel more like...me."

"But I thought they weren't you," I say.

"Right. They're aren't me, but now that they're around it's like I'm finally, you know, me: Camille."

I muse about this a moment and find I can't argue with how hanging out with her new pair of perky pals has made my sister not only want to see the world, but also become the best possible 36-B she can be. Yesterday, she got a new haircut, choppy and hip; tomorrow it's off with the children to a class in beginning guitar—a hint that Camille's childhood *that's-me!* fantasy (that of a fringe-dressed, hippie chick) may finally find expression. At forty? Yes, my sister's dreams, once delayed, her desires, never tried, are riding a tsunami of confidence unleashed by the swells that swell her sweaters.

And I am jealous. Of her power. Her pride. Her self-possession. Not to mention envious of all the trips and treks and sacks of luscious lingerie that's oh-so-fabulously French. Am I jealous of her breasts?

Not a chance. My bra is remaining a 34-A, thank you. When I see Camille considering her compelling cleavage with the bored detachment of a grocery clerk arranging his display of firm and flawless nectarines, I hug my own imperfect God-givens closer to my heart, live vicariously through my sister's adventures, and say to anyone who cares to ask (although unlike Camille I will not flash), make mine me.

Colette O'Connor is a beach-based writer currently either working hard or hardly working around the Monterey Bay area. She is (when working hard) editor in chief of Flying Adventures, *a travel and lifestyle magazine for aviators; when not, she spends time pining for Paris, pastries, and projects that cause her to ponder those wonders of life that inspire her to feel* how marvelous!

Acknowledgments

First and foremost, a big smooch-laden thanks to my guy James Gambrill: I couldn't have gotten through this project without your top-notch geek support, and I never would have survived those long hours in The Vortex without your love, patience, kindness, and tolerance for the Bad Juju. You are an exceptional man and my most perfect partner. I love you more than anything.

Next a tremendous thanks to Susan Brady who got me through some rough spots and busted ass when timelines got messy. You are truly amazing. Thanks to Larry Habegger, James O'Reilly, and Sean O'Reilly for taking a chance on a greenie like me. I couldn't have asked for a nicer or more talented bunch of chaps to work with. It's been a privilege and an honor. Thank you, Stefan Gutermuth for putting together a killer cover, and thanks to Dominic DeFazio and the Swimmers-on-Parade gals for the fabulous image.

Cheers to my Flamin' Ladies of the Red Hat Society, I'll never forget the Barnes & Noble reading—thongs for cheering me on! And a special thanks to my Three Queenies: Sharon, AlethaLou, and Shelley for keeping my spirits high and indulging with me in my favorite hobby: looking ridiculous in public. You rowdy broads light up my life. I love you all. And thanks to Guru G'Norm for the career forecast. Damn, you're good!

Thanks to flirt-e-boy PL at www.ijoke.tv for helping me get the word out. Whenever you want to talk travel show, you know where to find me. Thanks to the guys and gals over at *www. bootsnall.com* and *www.writtenroad.com* for your continued support of the series. Thanks to "Dougie Fresh" Springstead and the "J Crew" for letting me edit under sail. And to everyone I met during the Baja Ha Ha rally—it was nice to get some *actual* sand in my bra while I put this thing together. Thanks to Mom, Don, Elaine, Dad, Julie II, my brother Mike and my other brother Mike, Betsie, Leif, and Baby Bun, Ms. Maya, Jhoy and all my peeps in the Philippines, Thailand…around the world, the Bells, the Littles, Jen Farmer (and the wiener) Kenny, …and all my many friends and family for their love, support, and lifts to the airport. Didn't see your name here? Web over to www.juliaweiler.com for the extended version.

A special, super-sized thanks to the contributors and to everyone who sent in a submission for this book—we couldn't have done it without you. And last, but certainly not least, a HUGE shout out to the fabulous Ms. Jennifer L. Leo. Thank you for creating this hilarious and much loved series, and for allowing me to be a part of it. A millions kudos to you, my travelin' sistah—you are the brightest light in the sky. Rock on, Superstar, rock on!

—JW

I wouldn't have wanted to grow up anywhere other than right where I did—here at Travelers' Tales. From my young clueless days as an intern opening Larry's mail and creating his clip file, to touring the country for their hot pink and popular women's humor books, this decade-plus journey has been the best personal journey a hopeful writer and adventurer could ask for. The friendships and membership in the Travelers' Tales family has always meant more to me than the number of book sales, but it was both that have contributed to my current success. This time around, I only want to thank everyone at Travelers' Tales. James O'Reilly, Larry Habegger, Susan Brady, and Sean O'Reilly—please accept my lifelong appreciation for taking me in and treating me like one of your own, and especially investing in my career. Sometimes I feel like a sister, sometimes a daughter, but know that your long hours and 24/7 care has sculpted a woman my blood family is proud of. No matter where I end up or how far I travel, I will always feel at home when in your presence.

Additional gratitude to Cynthia Lamb and Stefan Gutermuth who work behind the scenes to make our books lovely inside and out. And much love to all the contributors in the series, the many bookstore event coordinators, and global fans who have given us a reason to keep at it. Most of all, ginormous thanks *to Julia Weiler, my undying appreciation for keeping this series alive and our Sand in My Bra fans awash with more inspiration and laughs in hand. You are a heroine in my history book, and I want to be the first to say that you're now a true branch in our TT family tree.*

—JLL

"Come Here" by Anne Merrigan published with permission from the author. Copyright © 2007 by Anne Merrigan.

"Booty Call" by Laurie Notaro excerpted from *We Thought You Would Be Prettier: True Tales of the Dorkiest Girl Alive* by Laurie Notaro. Copyright © 2005 by Laurie Notaro. Reprinted by permission of Villard, a division of Random House, Inc.

"Thar She Blows!" by Janna Cawrse published with permission from the author. Copyright © 2007 by Janna Cawrse.

"The Spa Who Loved Me" by Suz Redfearn published with permission from the author. Copyright © 2007 by Suz Redfearn.

"Honeymoon with Jaws" by Nancy Olds Smay published with permission from the author. Copyright © 2007 by Nancy Olds Smay.

"Going to Pot" by Susan Reinhardt excerpted from *Not Tonight, Honey: Wait 'til I'm a Size 6* by Susan Reinhardt. Copyright © 2005 by Susan Reinhardt. Reprinted by arrangement with Citadel Press/Kensington Publishing Corp. (www.kensingtonbooks.com). All rights reserved.

"Take Two Coke Hits and Call Me in the Morning" by Abbie Kozolchyk published with permission from the author. Copyright © 2007 by Abbie Kozolchyk.

"Oh, the Places She Will Go" by Rachel S. Thurston published with permission from the author. Copyright © 2007 by Rachel S. Thurston.

"When in Jordan" by Shari Caudron published with permission from the author. Copyright © 2007 by Shari Caudron.

"Once That Gun Goes Off" by Laura Katers published with permission from the author. Copyright © 2007 by Laura Katers.

"Mommy Nearest" by Beth E. Martinson published with permission from the author. Copyright © 2007 by Beth E. Martinson.

Additional Credits (arranged alphabetically by title)

Selection from "Eating My Own Words" by Tara L.M. Lowry published with permission from the author. Copyright © 2007 by Tara L.M. Lowry.

Selection from "Exploring New Heights" by Julia Weiler published with permission from the author. Copyright © 2007 by Julia Weiler.

Selection from "Family Vacation" by Anne Merrigan published with permission from the author. Copyright © 2007 by Anne Merrigan.

Selection from "I Need a Vacation" by Jennifer Graham published with permission from the author. Copyright © 2007 by Jennifer Graham.

Selection from "The Importance of Good Spanglish Skills" by Louise Schutte published with permission from the author. Copyright © 2007 by Louise Schutte.

Selection from "Killing Me Softly" by Andrea G. Fischer published with permission from the author. Copyright © 2007 by Andrea G. Fischer.

Selection from "Lost in Translation" by Kendra Lachniet published with permission from the author. Copyright © 2007 by Kendra Lachniet.

Selection from "Mama Knows Best" by Sharon Ashley published with permission from the author. Copyright © 2007 by Sharon Ashley.

Selection from "Meat Market Charades" by AlethaLou Harmon published with permission from the author. Copyright © 2007 by AlethaLou Harmon.

Selection from "My First Mutawa" by Anastasia Kozak published with permission from the author. Copyright © 2007 by Anastasia Kozak.

Selection from "Orion's Surprise" by Judy Edwards published with permission from the author. Copyright © 2006 by Judy Edwards.

Selection from "The Paris Dress Incident" by Tiffany Fisher published with permission from the author. Copyright © 2007 by Tiffany Fisher.

Selection from "A Philippine Farewell" by Julia Weiler published with permission from the author. Copyright © 2007 by Julia Weiler.

Selection from "Pumping the Turtle" by Louise Schutte published with permission from the author. Copyright © 2007 by Louise Schutte.

Selection from "Same, Same" by Julia Weiler published with permission from the author. Copyright © 2007 by Julia Weiler.

Selection from "Sherwood Forest" by Shelley Hughes published with permission from the author. Copyright © 2007 by Shelley Hughes.

Selection from "Surviving the Oregon Trail" by Betsey Lorenzen published with permission from the author. Copyright © 2007 by Betsey Lorenzen.

About the Editors

A chronic dabbler and incorrigible hyphenate, Julia Weiler has worked as a coffee demo girl, restaurant hostess, figure drawing model, artist, furniture designer, hot pepper farmer, veterinary technician, roofer, house flipper, filmmaker, photographer, writer, and most recently—book editor.

She is currently writing and illustrating a children's book tentatively titled *Curly J's Super-Size Book of Silly* or *Around the World in 80 Ways*, a collection of nonsense, rhymes, and poems for the young and the young at heart. She is also hard at work penning *Are You Still Here?,* the hilarious account of her seven-year quest to escape the American dream and become a global nomad.

A lifelong devotee to wanderlust and adventure, Julia and her husband, James Gambrill, will soon be renting out their house, farming out their cats, and hitting the road for their 'round the globe, Whirled View, video blogging tour. For the full scoop on their trip as well as travel reviews, news, vicarious thrills, and more tales from the trails than you can shake a passport at, visit www.juliaweiler.com.

Jennifer L. Leo is a magnet for misadventure and always ready to gamble on having a good time. She is the founding editor of the best-selling Travelers' Tales women's humor series, including the award-winning *Sand in My Bra, Whose Panties Are These?, The Thong Also Rises,* and *What Color is Your Jockstrap?* Her writing can be found in several books, magazines, and websites.

These days Jen is the featured blogger on the *Los Angeles Times* Travel Detectives: Daily Deal Blog. If she could be anywhere it'd be bodysurfing in Australia, eating shrimp tacos in Baja, or checking out a new hotel in Las Vegas.

Find out more about her work on www.Jenopolis.com.